JOURNEY *of*
1 0 0 YEARS

REFLECTIONS

on the CENTENNIAL

of PHILIPPINE

INDEPENDENCE

Edited by

Cecilia Manguerra Brainard

Edmundo F. Litton

Published by Philippine American Women Writers and Artists (P AWWA)
Distributed by
Philippine American Literary House
P. O. Box 5099
Santa Monica, CA 90409, U S A
http://www.palhbooks.com

AA CP, Inc.
P. O. Box 1587
San Mateo, CA 94401
1-800-874-2242

Tiboli Press
P. O. Box 347147
San Francisco, CA 94134
415-337-5550, e-mail: tiboli@mindspring.com

FIRST EDITION

Library of Congress Catalog Card number: 99-070272
Brainard Manguerra, Cecilia; and Litton, Edmundo F . (editors)
Journey of 1 0 0 Years: Reflections on the Centennial of Philippine Independence/Cecilia Manguerra Brainard and Edmundo F . Litton

      p.   cm.
      Includes biographical references (p.)
      I SBN 0-9632281-0-2
      1. History – Philippines 2. Filipino Americans

Cover design by Gloria Galang

ACKNOWLEDGEMENTS

Cecilia Manguerra Brainard: Photo by Doreen Stone; "Another Look at Magellan's Journey Around the World" from *Pacific Enterprise*, Volume 1, Number 1, 1998.

Luisa A. Igloria: "Radicalizing the Image: The Revolutionary Icons in Contemporary Philippine Poetry by Women" first presented at the Loyola Marymount University/Philippine American Women Writers and Artists conference, *Journey of 100 Years: The Philippine Experience*, April, 1998.

Paulino Lim, Jr. : "Finding Your Voice: The Bilingual Writer's Dilemma" first presented at the Loyola Marymount University/Philippine American Women Writers and Artists conference, *Journey of 100 Years: The Philippine Experience*, April, 1998.

Edmundo F. Litton: "The Marriage of Maria Clara and Uncle Sam: Colonialism and the Education of Filipinos" first presented at the Loyola Marymount University/Philippine American Women Writers and Artists conference, *Journey of 100 Years: The Philippine Experience*, April, 1998.

Susan N. Montepio: "Folklore and Creative Aging among Elderly Filipinos in Los Angeles" first presented at the Loyola Marymount University/Philippine American Women Writers and Artists conference, *Journey of 100 Years: The Philippine Experience*, April, 1998.

Herminia Meñez: "The Tausug Ballad of Putli Isara" first presented at the Loyola Marymount University/Philippine American Women Writers and Artists conference, *Journey of 100 Years: The Philippine Experience*, April, 1998.

Felice Prudente Sta. Maria : Photos courtesy of Studio 5.

Nadine Sarreal: "Writing Fast, Writing Quickly – Hear Your Voice or Drop That Stereotype" first presented at the Loyola Marymount University/Philippine American Women Writers and Artists conference, *Journey of 100 Years: The Philippine Experience*, April, 1998.

John Silva: Photos courtesy of John Silva.

The editors wish to acknowledge the support of the California Arts Council whose Multicultural Entry Grant made this book possible.

Additionally, the editors would like to express their appreciation to the following individuals and departments at Loyola Marymount University for co-sponsoring the conference:

> Fr. Thomas P. O'Malley, President
> Dr. Lane Bove, Vice President for Student Affairs
> Dr. Joseph Jabbra, Academic Vice President
> Mr. Marshall Sauceda, Assistant Dean for Student
>   Development Services
> Fr. Richard Daly, Center for Asian Business
> Dr. Linda Bannister, English Department
> Fr. Albert Koppes, O. Carm., School of Education
> Dr. Jennifer Abe Kim, Asian Pacific American Studies

TABLE OF CONTENTS

Acknowledgements iii

Introduction vii
Cecilia Manguerra Brainard and Edmundo F. Litton

I : 1 0 0 Years of Philippine History

· Another Look at Magellan's Journey Around the World 3
Cecilia Manguerra Brainard

· *Los Agraviados*: Another Side of 1898 19
Damon Woods

· Political Culture and Imperialism: The Philippine Experience 33
Elizabeth Pastores-Palffy

· Christianity in the Philippines: Some Reflections on
a Spanish Legacy 57
Santiago Sia

· Of Photographs and Country Roads 69
John Silva

II : 1 0 0 Years of Philippine Education

· The Marriage of Maria Clara and Uncle Sam:
Colonialism and the Education of Filipinos 83
Edmundo F. Litton

· Language of Instruction in the Philippines During the
Twentieth Century: Policies, Orientations,
and Future Directions 97
Rosita G. Galang

· Amazing Space: Reviewing the Role of Cultural
Environment Development Toward Values Education 119
Felice Prudente Sta. Maria

III : 1 0 0 Years of Filipino Presence in America

· The Filipino Diaspora and the Centenary of
the Philippine Revolution 135
E. San Juan, Jr.

· The Manongs: Past and Present 159
Susan Evangelista

· Temple Street: Filipino Life in Los Angeles 169
Valorie Slaughter Bejarano

· Folklore and Creative Aging Among Elderly Filipinos
in Los Angeles 175
Susan N. Montepio

IV : 1 0 0 Years of Filipino Literature (Oral and Written)

· The Tausug Ballad of Putli Isara: Colonialism,
Gender, and Religion 189
Herminia Meñez

· Vibrant, Vulgar, Vigilant: A History of the Filipino Newspaper 203
Ruel de Vera

· Finding Your Voice: The Bilingual Writer's Dilemma 217
Paulino Lim, Jr.

· Writing Fast, Writing Quickly—Hear Your Voice or
Drop That Stereotype 231
Nadine Sarreal

· Radicalizing the Image: The Revolutionary Philippine
Feminine in Poetry 239
Luisa A. Igloria

About the Authors 253

INTRODUCTION

Cecilia Manguerra Brainard
and Edmundo F. Litton

On June 12, 1998, the Philippines celebrated one hundred years of independence from Spain after more than three centuries of colonization. Since the momentous occasion when General Emilio Aguinaldo declared the birth of the Philippine Republic, the Philippines has undergone numerous changes. At the turn of the century and as part of America's experimentation with imperialism, the Philippines became a colony of the United States; and it embarked on a convoluted relationship with the United States that would affect every fabric of life for all Filipinos including, politics, migration, culture, education, and language.

In 1941, the Philippines became a major player during World War II in the Pacific. In 1946, America granted independence to war-torn Philippines. For the next decades, the Philippines rebuilt itself and even experienced a time of prosperity, only to suffer political turmoil during the Marcos era. Martial Law of 1972 marked a low-point in Philippine politics, with the Filipino people deprived of their basic rights. The media was censored and opposition leaders were killed, jailed, or driven away to exile in other countries. It was not until the dramatic martyrdom of Benigno Aquino, Jr., on August 21, 1983 at the Manila International Airport, when the Filipino people declared, *"Tama na!* — Enough!' and began their peaceful revolt that culminated in the "People Power" overthrow of the government of Ferdinand Marcos on February 1986. Once again, the Philippines reinstalled democracy and set about rebuilding the country. Still another event that occurred was the eruption of Mount Pinatubo in 1991 that subsequently destroyed the American military bases in the Philippines—ending years of America's presence in the Philippines.

These historic events of the past 100 years made deep and lasting changes on the Philippines and the Filipino people—topics discussed by the contributors of this book.

This book is a product of a collaborative effort of Philippine American Women Writers and Artists (PAWWA) and Asian Pacific Student Services of Loyola Marymount University, Los Angeles, California. Specifically, it is an offshoot of the one-day conference— *Journey of 100 Years: The Philippine Experience*—held by PAWWA and Asian Pacific Student Services last April 14, 1998. The conference and book are our way of participating in the worldwide celebration of the Philippine Centennial. We used the papers presented at the conference as the core of this book; and we also invited highly respected scholars who were unable to attend the conference to submit works reflective of the Centennial. It is our hope that this book documents the thoughts of some of the best minds on this important milestone—the Philippine Centennial.

The contributors for this book come from diverse backgrounds. Some of them are literary authors, educators, historians, folklorists, and journalists. Thus, the style of each chapter is unique to the author's experience and academic discipline. We believe that the diversity in style and viewpoints makes this collection particularly interesting.

We would like to note that this book is PAWWA's swan song project. PAWWA has a colorful background. In 1991, a small group of Filipina writers in Southern California formed Philippine American Women Writers and Artists (PAWWA). There were only seven in the group and the group was adamant about remaining seven. Small though the group was, the seven women had big dreams of providing community service and helping other writers and artists. PAWWA co-sponsored numerous literary events and lectures; and it encouraged the creation of PAWWA-North, another group of Filipina writers from Northern California. PAWWA also sponsored Filipina writers in a Community Access Scholarship Program at the Writers Program at UCLA Extension.

For six years, PAWWA received the highly competitive Multicultural Entry Grant from California Arts Council. PAWWA stretched that funding to help publish some works: *Seven Stories from Seven Sisters: A Collection of Philippine Folktales, The Beginning and Other Asian Folktales, A Directory of Philippine American Women Writers and Artists,* a newsletter, and finally this anthology. When PAWWA's CAC funding ran out in June, 1998, the remaining members of PAWWA decided to move on, and PAWWA was dissolved.

But despite the fact that PAWWA no longer exists, we hope that this final book project of PAWWA and Asian Pacific Student Servies at Loyola Marymount University can take on a life of its own to be read and appreciated by educators, Filipino youth, and the general readership.

100 Years of Philippine History

{ I }

ANOTHER LOOK AT MAGELLAN'S JOURNEY AROUND THE WORLD

Cecilia Manguerra Brainard

The centennial celebration of Philippine Independence from Spain is a good occasion to look once again at that historic moment over four centuries ago when the Spanish galleons first sailed into the Philippines back in 1521.

I will be the first to admit that for years I believed what many people probably still say today, and that is that the Portuguese explorer, Ferdinand Magellan, sailing for the Spanish crown, discovered the Philippines. Magellan was the first person to circumnavigate the world, I used to say. Only as a grown woman did I stop to think that Magellan had not "discovered" the Philippines; people had lived in the archipelago for centuries before his three ships showed up—the *Trinidad*, the *Victoria*, and the *Concepcion*—to irrevocably change the lives of the people born there.

It also took a while before I realized that Magellan was not the first to go around the world. The first European given this credit is Juan Sebastian del Cano, one of Magellan's crewmen, who ironically had participated in an aborted mutiny against the iron-fisted Magellan, but who later led the battered *Victoria* back to Seville from where they had departed. Del Cano and seventeen others, a ragtag group, marched barefoot to the churches of Santa Maria de la Victoria and Santa Maria Antiqua to thank God that they, out of 265 men, had survived the tortuous three-year journey.

Even longer did it take me to understand that the first documented person to circumnavigate the world was Magellan's Malay slave. "What an amazing moment, one of the most remarkable in the history of mankind!" wrote Stefan Zweig, author of *Conqueror of the Seas,* a biography of Magellan. "For the first time since our planet had begun to spin upon its axis and to circle in its orbit, a living man, himself circling that planet, had got back to his homeland. No matter that he was an underling, a slave, for his significance lies in his fate and not in his personality. He is known to us only by his slave-name Enrique; but we know, likewise, that he was torn from his home upon the island of Sumatra, was bought by Magellan in Malacca, was taken by his master to India, to Africa, and to Lisbon; traveled thence to Brazil and to Patagonia; and first of all the population of the world, traversing the oceans, circling the globe, he returned to the region where men spoke a familiar tongue. Having made acquaintance on the way with hundreds of peoples and tribes and races, each of which had a different way of communicating thought, he had got back to his own folk, whom he could understand and who could understand him."

Most historical documents have assigned Enrique a background role, often summing him up as a footnote. However, if one reads between the lines one can see that Enrique was a major player in the events that took place between 1519 to 1521 in Spain, the high seas, and the archipelago later called *Las Islas Filipinas*. My interest in Enrique lies in the fact that he spoke the same language as the people of Cebu, which in my eyes makes him my *kababayan*. I was, after all, born in Cebu, the land of the *pintados* (tattooed), a major turning point for Magellan and his crew.

Let me backtrack here and start from the beginning.

Ferdinand Magellan, also known by his Portuguese name of Fernao de Magalhaes e Sousa, was born about 1480 in Northern Portugal. At the time, the Portuguese were eager to corner the spice market. They sought a seaward route to the East Indies to transport the coveted spices from the east to Portugal. They were also engaged in an expansionist program whereby they captured trading posts along the African coasts all the way to the Far East. Magellan served in several East Indies expeditions—wars, one may more accurately say.

Several important events happened during those military forays: Magellan received several wounds, one in particular was a lance-thrust to his left knee so that he walked with a limp; second, Magellan struck a close friendship with Fernando Serrao, who later deserted the Portuguese navy to live in Ternate as captain-general of the local king. In exchange for his services as military advisor, the King of Ternate gave Serrao his own house with slaves. Serrao acquired a native wife and had children, and overall he lived an idyllic life, prompting Zweig to comment, "Down to the day of his death, nine years later, the refugee from Western civilization never quitted the Sunda Islands, being not perhaps the most heroic, but probably the wisest and the happiest of the conquistadors and capitanos of the Great Age of Portugal."

After seven years in the East Indies, Magellan served in Africa where he and another officer had the important job of looking after the horses and cattle taken from the Moors. An incident occurred where a dozen sheep vanished and Magellan and his companion were accused of secretly reselling the sheep back to the Moors or allowing the enemy to steal the sheep. Magellan returned to Portugal to clear his name. His encounter with the king regarding this matter and a subsequent meeting regarding his proposal to go westward to reach the Indies were disagreeable ones. Magellan finally asked King Manuel permission to serve another country. In an act that had deep repercussions, the king did not object. After a year of quietly gathering navigational information in Lisbon, Magellan with Enrique in tow, left for Seville. There he quickly married Beatriz Barboza, who as daughter of the alcalde of the Seville arsenal and Knight of the Order of Santiago, provided Magellan the necessary connections to make his dream a reality.

Magellan's idea was to sail west to reach the Indies, a vision inspired by his friend Serrao's enthusiasm for his adopted home: "I have found here a new world, richer and greater than that of Vasco da Gama." Serrao's letters gave precise geographical and statistical information about the Sunda Islands, which triggered in Magellan the thought that perhaps it was closer to go westward, instead of eastward, from Portugal to reach these same islands. It was this proposal that he parlayed to the Spaniards; and Magellan being the thorough person that he was had even astonished the Privy Council (a group of four councillors of the King of Spain) by presenting Enrique, a woman from Sumatra, and a pair of "Orientals," the sight of whom made the fabled Spice Islands that much more desirable to the Spaniards.

The Spaniards financed the journey, not out of love for this Portuguese navigator whom many perceived as a traitor to his own country, but out of love for money. So expensive were spices in Europe that peppercorn was worth its weight in silver and was sold corn by corn. The way politics was at that time, Portugal owned the East, and Spain owned the West. If Spain could find a backdoor to the East via the West, they would have followed the rules and still acquire their spices. Magellan's proposal was accepted, but to check the Portuguese navigator, four high-ranking Spaniards were assigned captains of four of the five ships.

On August 10, 1519, the flagship *Trinidad* along with the *San Antonio, Victoria, Santiago,* and *Concepcion* sailed down the Guadalquivir Canal and on to the Atlantic. Members of the crew included Spanish, Italian, French, Portuguese, Greek, Catalan, German, and two Malays (one of them Enrique). With a few exceptions, the crew was a rough, uneducated bunch, who basically had little to lose. "Weeks and weeks had passed before they had been gathered from the alleys and the taverns. They arrived in rags, dirty and undisciplined," wrote Zweig.

Surprisingly, one of the passengers was an Italian nobleman, Antonio Pigafetta, around 28 years of age, whose wanderlust compelled him to join the expedition. Most of what we know about that historic trip came from Pigafetta who was like a camera recording what transpired in his famous journals.

One of the more monumental events that occurred was the mutiny led by the Spanish captains. Early in the trip, Magellan had been warned that the Spanish leaders would rebel if they did not get their way. At Port San Julian, off the coast of South America, they staged their rebellion and demanded to turn back. Magellan dealt with the matter swiftly and surely. Pigafetta summed up the event in few but terse lines:

"We remained about five months in the port of Saint Julian. And as soon as we had entered the port, the captains of the other four vessels treacherously wanted to kill the Captain General. And they were Juan de Caragena, the treasurer Luis de Mendoza, Antonio de Coca, and Gaspar de Quesada. The treachery having been discovered, the treasurer was killed (by dagger blows) and quartered. Gaspar de Quesada was beheaded and quartered. Juan de Cartagena was left behind in Patagonia with a priest."

Very slowly, very painfully, the journey continued. They lost one ship, another abandoned them, and down to three ships, they traversed the "paso"—the Strait of Magellan—on to the huge body of water they called Pacific because of its unrelenting tranquility. Pigafetta reported: "We sailed out from this strait into the Pacific Sea on the 28th of November in the year 1520, and we were three months and twenty days without eating anything (i.e., fresh food), and we ate biscuit, and when there was no more of that we ate the crumbs which were full of maggots and smelled strongly of mouse urine. We drank yellow water, already several days putrid. And we ate some of the hides that were on the largest shroud to keep it from breaking and that were very much toughened by the sun, rain and winds. And we softened them in the sea for four or five days, and then we put them in a pot over the fire and ate them and also much sawdust. A mouse would bring half a ducat or a ducat. The gums of some of the men swelled over their upper and lower teeth, so that they could not eat and so they died. And nineteen men died from that sickness . . . "

They came upon two barren islands, which offered them nothing and which they called the Unfortunate Islands; but they had better luck on March 6, when they found a lush island, which they called Ladrones (Guam) because the natives stole their things. It had never occurred to Magellan that they too were guilty of stealing, that the very notion of splitting the world into two—one-half for Portugal, the other half for Spain, that they were "ladrones" all the same; and so with vengeance, Magellan and 40 men taught the natives a bitter lesson. They burned a village of 40 or 50 houses and killed people. "When our men hit some of them with arrows that passed through their flanks from one side to the other, they pulled out the arrows so that they could look at them; and when they had pulled them out they wondered greatly and so they died,"—from Pigafetta again.

March 16, 1521, was the day Magellan's expedition hit Samar, which was populated with friendly people. Refreshed and delighted at the "reasonable" natives, they proceeded to explore the surrounding islands, which Magellan named the Archipelago of San Lazarus, but which was later renamed the Philippines.

And now we come to the part of the story where Enrique plays an important role. Despite his lowly position, Enrique was probably the man closest to Magellan. Acquired by Magellan when he was only 16 or 17, Enrique had spent over a decade as Magellan's companion. When Magellan was one of the conquerors of Malacca in 1511, there was Enrique; when he was disgraced in Africa, there was Enrique; when he returned to Lisbon and was so poor he had to endure the tremendous bureaucracy to increase his pension by a few maravedis, there was Enrique; when he went to Seville to play the necessary game to get his expedition financed, there was Enrique; and when he finally sailed westward to waters and lands unknown, there was Enrique.

The slave/master relationship must have diminished in time, so that Magellan, before leaving Seville, wrote in his last will and testament: "I declare and ordain that from the day of my death thenceforward for ever, my captured slave Enrique, mulatto, native of the city of Malacca, of the age of twenty-six years more or less, shall be free and manumitted, and quit, exempt, and relieved of every obligation of slavery and subjection, that he may act as he desires and thinks fit; and I desire that of my estate there may be given to the said Enrique the sum of ten thousand maravedis in money for his support; and this manumission I grant because he is a Christian and that he may pray to God for my soul."

On March 28, by Pigafetta's reckoning, the explorers came to an island (in northeastern Mindanao) where Enrique could understand the people's language and be understood as well. "They saw a fire on the island," Pigafetta recorded, "and they saw a small boat, and eight men in it, which approached the Captain's ship, and a slave from Sumatra, which is called Traporbane, being in the Captain's ship, spoke, and they understood at once, and quickly came to the port of the ship, and did not want to board her."

This was a landmark moment not only to Enrique but also to Magellan who must have realized how close he was to reaching the Spice Islands and who understood the historic significance of his journey.

History books give little information about Enrique, but he had probably been yanked away from his village by slave traders when he was young. For centuries, slave traders sailing in their prahus raided coastal villages and kidnapped people, some of them mere babies. They were sold in slave markets in the same way Enrique was sold in Malacca. As Magellan's slave, he traveled far from his own people to places where the weather, people, and foods were alien to him. How strange he must have felt when Europeans looked at him as if he were an exotic being or a freak. How cold he must have felt when the clammy Iberian winters arrived. How surprised he probably was to note that Europeans rarely bathed unlike his own people who bathed daily in rivers and in the sea. How lonely he must have felt when he found no one of his own kind to talk to.

When they crossed the Pacific, and even before they reached the Ladrones, Enrique must have sensed a shift in humidity, a change in weather, signalling that they were entering the tropics; memories of his past must have drifted back to him. When he saw the people of Guam, his pulse must have quickened at the sight of their brown faces; and in the northeastern part of Mindanao when at last he met people with whom he could converse with, his happiness must have been boundless.

They were "handsome people," wrote Pigafetta about them. "They go about naked and painted (tattooed); they wear a piece of tree-cloth over their shameful parts. The women are clothed from the waist down, with black hair reaching the ground. Their ears are pierced and full of gold. All day long these people chew a fruit that they call areca, and it is like a pear . . . And when they have chewed it well, they spit it out, and it makes their mouths red."

Using Enrique as interpreter, Magellan inquired where the best place was to stock-up on food and supplies. The local kings named three places, one of them (and the largest) Cebu.

Magellan and his crew went there. "On the seventh day of April at midday, we entered the port of Zubu (Cebu), passing by many villages, and seeing many houses on tree trunks, and we approached the city. And the Captain ordered the ships to approach, and to lower their sails and arrange themselves in battle formation and to fire all their guns. Wherefore these people were greatly frightened."

Pigafetta recorded the events that led to Magellan's death as follows:

Instead of stocking up on their necessities and leaving for the Moluccas, Magellan and his crew tarried in Cebu where Magellan befriended the king. They exchanged gifts; they had a blood pact. The King of Cebu, called Rajah Humabon, even gave the Spaniards a place in the square to bury their dead. The Spanish crew traded their goods in Cebu's market. Magellan talked of Christianity and insisted that the people burn their idols "made of wood, hollowed out behind . . . with bare arms and the feet turned up with bare legs, and a large face, with four teeth as large as boar tusks and . . . painted all over."

Rajah Humabon, his queen, and many of their subjects were baptized. The queen, by the way, received a statue of the Child Jesus, which Magellan did not perceive as an idol. This same statue still exists today and is revered as the Santo Niño de Cebu.

Despite the seeming acquiescence of the people from Cebu, a village from nearby Mactan Island refused to obey Magellan. As a result of this defiance, the Spaniards burned down that village and set up a cross there.

Shortly after, Zula, the chief of Mactan, sent one of his sons to Magellan to ask for one boatload of men to help him fight Lapulapu who refused to obey the king of Spain.

Magellan sent three boats with 60 men; and he himself would fight to teach these natives a lesson. Even though Rajah Humabon was present with 20 or 30 boats, Magellan told him to stay put and watch how Spaniards fought. The Portuguese veteran of many wars was counting on European cannons, muskets, and crossbows overpowering the natives with their charred bamboo and charred pointed stakes. Magellan and his crew had done this many times before: go ashore, burn the village, kill people, and get back on their ships; they had done it effectively at the Ladrones. However, at this battle there was one matter that Magellan had neglected, a question of logistics. He had not figured on when low tide or high tide was in this particular island. Specifically, he was unaware that the shallow coral reefs of Mactan extended far during low tide and boats could not navigate these extremely shallow waters. The coral reefs were as good a barrier as a moat, or a high wall, or cliff. Magellan discovered this fact too late, when he and his men leaped into the shallow water and had to wade a long distance so that their boats were far away. The shooting of the muskets and crossbows from the boats were totally ineffective, a fact that Lapulapu and his 1,500 men quickly noted and which made them shout louder and hurl their weapons at Magellan.

Hoping to frighten the natives, Magellan ordered some men to burn their houses. But this only infuriated the natives further. "And so great a number came upon us that they pierced the right leg of the Captain with a poisoned arrow, wherefore he ordered that they gradually retreat, and they would follow them, and six or eight remained with the Captain. These people aimed only at their legs because they were not covered with armor. And they had so many spears, darts and stones that Magellan's soldiers could not withstand them, and the artillery of the fleet was so far away that it could not help them. And our men withdrew to the shore, fighting all the while, even up to their knees in water, and the natives recovered their own spears four or five times in order to throw them at us. They recognized the Captain and so many assailed him that twice they knocked his sallet from his head. And he, like a good knight, continued to stand firm with a few others, and they fought thus for more than an hour and refused to retreat. An Indian threw his bamboo spear into his face and he immediately killed him with his own spear and it remained in the Indian's body. And the Captain tried to draw his sword and was able to draw it only half way, because he had been wounded in the arm with a spear. When our men saw this they turned their back and made their way to the ships, still pursued with lances and darts until they were out of sight, and they killed their native guide," lamented the Italian who hero-worshipped Magellan.

Eight Europeans died with Magellan; four Christian Indians died from friendly fire from the Spanish ships; fifteen of Lapulapu's men died.

What follows intrigues me and makes me wonder if the native chiefs had conspired to get rid of the European invaders, especially after hearing stories from a Moorish merchant about the horrors the Portuguese had committed during the conquer of Calicut, India, and Malacca. Enrique, one of those who had participated in the Mactan battle, had been wounded. He lay bedridden, nursing his wounds and mourning Magellan's death, when along came Duarte Barbosa, Magellan's brother-in-law, to command Enrique to get up and interpret for him. Barbosa, in a vile mood because of the recent disaster, told Enrique that although Magellan was dead, this did not mean he was a freeman, and that when they returned to Spain, he would have to serve Magellan's widow Beatriz. Barbosa threatened to whip Enrique if he did not go ashore as he commanded. Barbosa's ill temper would cost him his life. Enrique, who must have known of Magellan's last will and testament, hid his anger. Mustering whatever dignity he could, he rose and acted as if he did not mind Barbosa's words, and then he went ashore and told Rajah Humabon that the Spaniards were planning to leave soon, but that he ought to take the Spanish ships and merchandise.

Humabon, who had been recorded by Pigafetta all along as Magellan's ally, sent word to the Spaniards that he had ready the jewels for the King of Spain, and he invited them to eat with him. Twenty-nine crewmen walked straight into the trap, Barbosa among them. At an appointed time, Humabon ordered his men to attack the Europeans. The remaining crew, on learning what was happening, prepared to sail away. It was a disgraceful, hasty departure. Just as they had abandoned Magellan's body in Mactan, they abandoned their fellow crewmen on Cebu. One of them, Jaoa Serrao, had managed to flee to the beach, where he begged his companions to ransom him, a plea that was ignored. Only Enrique survived the massacre; and Pigafetta made note of Enrique's "treachery."

The story continued: they had to burn one more ship, *Concepcion*, and they took a circuitous route to the Indies, stocked up on spices, and surprisingly the solitary ship *Victoria* that made it back to Seville on September 8, 1521, still made money from its spice cargo.

But what happened in Cebu and Mactan? Something more happened than was apparent to Pigafetta. My premise is that, the chieftains of Cebu and Mactan did not want the Spaniards there. Magellan had arrived shooting bombards and swinging his weight; he had refused to pay the customary tribute to Humabon; he had forced the people to get rid of their old religion; his men had raped local women; all in all they had conducted themselves in a barbaric way and, playing the diplomat, Humabon had gritted his teeth, hoping they would leave soon for the Moluccas or wherever their destination was. Seeing that they were hanging around and had even burned a village in Mactan, and warned by the Moorish merchant of Portuguese barbarity, Humabon and other chiefs had pulled their forces together and duped Magellan and his men into that coral reef trap. One thousand five hundred men waited for Magellan and his men—this large number was a result of an amalgam of armies from the various chiefs, not one chief's army.

How surprising that Humabon, supposedly an ally of Magellan, had not warned the Portuguese about the tides and coral reefs; how surprising the massacre the day after Magellan's death; how interesting the display of hatred for the religion forced on them by the

Portuguese: "Our men see from the ships that the beautiful cross which they had hoisted on a tree was hurled to the ground, and kicked to pieces by the savages with great fury," reported Maximilian of Transylvania, who recorded another historical account of the famous journey.

As far as Enrique was concerned, I suspect he may have sensed that Humabon had not been a true friend to Magellan. He may have warned Magellan, but Portuguese arrogance may have gotten the better of the navigator who may have said, wait and see how he, Magellan, would bend the will of Humabon and his people. Perhaps Enrique may even have believed that Humabon had been bullied into compliance; but when his master was slain on the shores of Mactan, Enrique understood it all. After the battle, he assessed the situation, which was: Magellan and the whole lot of them had been tricked by the local people; but Enrique also knew that the Spanish crew had not been nice, that they had kidnapped and killed people, raped women; and he knew that if he continued on that journey, he would probably die from the incompetence of the new captain, and if he did make it back to Seville, what faced him was a life of slavery for Beatriz. Cold dreary winters; cold harsh words; Barbosa had already given him a sample with his screaming and threatening to beat him. No thank you, must have been Enrique's conclusion. And so he left the *Trinidad* and went ashore and threw his lot on the people who were more kin to him that those he had just left behind, and he made his deal with Humabon.

Was it treachery? Or was it a matter of survival? Was it nationalism? It all depends what your point of view is in terms of assessing the actions of those peoples in Cebu and Mactan and Enrique. As one descended from those *Pintados,* I look at the events of 1521 as early resistance to foreign domination. It was not petty tribal warfare that killed Magellan and drove the Spaniards away, but a concerted military effort by people who did not wish to be subjugated.

Of course another question enters my mind: why have historians always referred to Magellan's death as a result of his involvement in tribal warfare? Was it very difficult for Pigafetta and other Western historians to consider that Magellan had been outwitted by the peoples of Cebu and Mactan, that in fact the people there had not wanted Spanish presence from the very start? Was it too humiliating to say that what occurred was a real battle, a war, the local people versus the Spaniards, and that in this battle, the Spaniards lost? Or was it a political maneuver to say that the people welcomed them and Catholicism so that they could more easily finance future expeditions to the Philippines?

I leave it up to the readers to reflect and answer these questions.

REFERENCES

Nowell, Charles E., ed. 1962. *Magellan's Voyage Around the World: Three Contemporary Accounts.* Evanston: Northwestern University Press.

Paige, Paula Spurlin, trans. 1969. *The Voyage of Magellan: The Journal of Antonio Pigafetta.* Englewood Cliffs, New Jersey: Prentice-Hall.

Villiers, Alan. 1976. "First Voyage Around the World." *National Geographic* 149(6)

Zweig, Stefan. 1938. *Conqueror of the Seas: The Story of Magellan.* New York: The Viking Press.

LOS AGRAVIADOS:
ANOTHER SIDE OF 1898

Damon Woods

In 1898, various parts of the province of Pangasinan were under the control of at least three different powers: the Spaniards, the Revolutionaries, and *Los Agraviados*. Most are familiar with the revolution which began in 1896, but have not heard of the *Agraviados*. From Lapu-lapu to the Tondo Conspiracy of 1587, from the babaylan Tamblot of Bohol and his revolt in 1621 to the Pampanga Revolt of 1660, from the revolt in the Tagalog provinces in 1745 to Diego Silang in 1762, there has been a radical tradition in Philippine history. The revolution is but the most remembered of movements and events of that time, in part, because it was political and nationalistic, and therefore more recognizable to twentieth-century Filipinos. But who were these people—the *Agraviados*? Why were they not a part of the Philippine Revolution? What is their story? How do they compare to the *Katipunan* and the Philippine Revolution?

The year 1872 was significant in Philippine history. It was the year which saw the Cavite Mutiny, the resulting execution of the three Filipino priests, Mariano Gomes, José Burgos, and Jacinto Zamora, and the entrance of an eleven-year-old boy named José Rizal into the Ateneo de Manila. Less known about 1872 is the founding of a religious association at the Santo Domingo convent in Manila. Its stated purposes were threefold: promote Christian virtues, particularly chastity; encourage devotion to the Virgin Mary; increase popular participation in church functions. The name of this new association was *Guardia de Honor de Maria* (Mary's Honor Guard) or *Guardias de Honor de Nuestra Señora del Rosario* (Honor Guards for Our Lady of the Rosary). This served as the beginning of the *Los Agraviados*.[1]

The requirements for joining were minimal: one had to swear to abide by the regulations and then his or her name was added to an authorized list. Those who joined were given certificates and colorful scapularies, two strips of cloth joined across the shoulders and hanging down in front. To remain in good standing, members had to recite the Rosary at assigned hours each day, as well as accompany the image of the Virgin during processions.

The movement exploded, in Manila and in the provinces (thus it was not a strictly rural movement). The Dominicans were not able to control the flourishing institution. With a shortage of priests in the Ilocos region, the pastors had little time to shepherd or guide the *Guardia de Honor*. They saw to the compiling of membership lists and selected prominent townsmen to serve as local leaders; but over-all "they left the organization to its own devices." (Sturtevant, 1976:98)

By 1880, the same year Graciano Lopez Jaena, the first editor of *La Solidaridad*, had to leave the Philippines, "the movement threatened to get out of hand. Hundreds of villagers were proclaiming themselves *Guardias de Honor* without clerical sanction." (Sturtevant, 1976: 98) It was reported that many began to incorporate pagan rites into their own daily worship. The Spanish clergy urged that the sodality be ended. In 1882, the year José Rizal left the Philippines, recognition was withdrawn from the Ilocano chapters.

Rather than dampening enthusiasm, this action resulted in additional momentum for the association, which was now free from the controls of the Church. Pangasinan became the center for activities, in part, because it was the locale of the famous shrine to the Virgin in Manaoag. At this point, Julian Baltazar, a long-time resident of Urdaneta, became the organization's leader. Baltazar had a reputation as a powerful *anitero* (animist) and a faith healer. He was called Apo Láqui (Mister Grandfather) by his followers. It was also reported that his blind wife, known as Apo Bae, also had supernatural powers; she was known as the "goddess." Under their control, the *Guardia de Honor* became a millennarian movement.

A dramatic change came in 1886, one year before the printing of *Noli Me Tangere*. Baltazar proclaimed the approach of Judgment Day. He stated that a flood would wipe out mankind, but that the virtuous might escape. Such escape was only possible on Santa Ana, a small island in the Agno River, near Asingan. "Accepting the warning as divine revelation, Ilocano villagers abandoned their farms and fishing boats and fled to safety." (Sturtevant, 1976:99) By the end of the dry season, thousands were camped along the Agno and the Spanish authorities feared that either a spiritual or physical disaster might result. The governor of Pangasinan ordered the Guardia Civil to clear out all those not from that area. The rains came and it was a normal rainy season.

Baltazar and his wife returned to Urdaneta. Their home became the center of the movement between 1886 and 1896.

At times Urdaneta resembled a gypsy encampment overflowing with foot-loose provincianos, scampering children, creaking carts and raucous animals. The peasant caravans arrived and departed according to rhythms beyond the ken of curious outsiders. Most of the pilgrims, however, paused at Baltazar's house to pay homage on their way or from the Dominican shrine in neighboring Manaoag. There, overworked clerical residents found it almost impossible to keep pace with demands for special masses. Once more scapularies and rosaries began to appear in unprecedented numbers. The Guardia's resurgence, linked to rumors concerning Mrs. Baltazar's growing powers, convinced Pangasinan's churchmen that the time had come to reassert ecclesiastical control. (Sturtevant, 1976:99-100)

Investigation revealed that the movement was far larger than believed. Urdaneta's parish priest, Father Cipriano Pampliega, urged secular authorities to take action. Baltazar was summoned to Lingayen to appear before the governor. Convinced that the issue was purely religious, the governor told Baltazar to behave himself and go home. This successful encounter with the government only enhanced Baltazar's image.

In November, 1896, Mrs. Baltazar passed away. Soon after, stories began to spread about the appearance of her spirit near several watering places. It was said that she was bestowing curative powers to the town's wells and fountains.

In 1897, Baltazar remarried, reorganized the *Guardia de Honor,* and selected a successor, Antonio Valdes. Baltazar and his followers moved to Montiel, a remote sitio. The community of members was renamed *Cabaruan* (Renewal). External events were beginning to affect the group. For two years, members of the *Katipunan* in Pangasinan had courted the movement, hoping to win their support in the fight against Spain. Baltazar refused, "disturbed by the Katipunan's Tagalog leadership and repelled by its secularism." (Sturtevant, 1976:101)

However, the deteriorating political situation called for some action. Firm in his desire to remain neutral, Baltazar had Valdes organize military units for the protection of the *Guardia de Honor*. Bolo companies were organized. Neutrality was impossible. Valdes secured firearms and raided some Spanish outposts. This provoked Spanish response, both ecclesiastical and civil. The Bishop of Vigan designated the *Guardia* a dangerous heresy and Baltazar was arrested by the civil authorities. The members were compelled to disperse. Valdes was on the run, rallying Apo Laqui's followers, and opposing all outsiders. He and his men became skilled fighters. Even when the Revolutionaries and the Spaniards declared the Biyak-na-bato truce, the *Guardia de Honor* continued to do battle.

Baltazar was released in December, 1897, as the result of the general amnesty. The seven months in prison had done its damage and the leader of the *Guardia de Honor* died before the end of the year. Valdes blamed outsiders for his death and saw both the Spaniards and the revolutionaries as the enemy. Retreating into the mountains, they began to call themselves *Los Agraviados* (the oppressed) and they attacked towns and haciendas. In contrast to the situation in Tagalog provinces where there were two choices—the Spaniards and the *Katipuneros*—the *Agraviados* became one of three alternatives in Pangasinan. In the middle of 1898, the revolutionaries controlled the towns, but the *Agraviados* ruled the barrios. Seeking to break the stalemate, Valdes stepped forward as the champion of the Catholic church. He ordered his followers to help Spanish friars when they came under attack; they helped to release some from captivity and escorted some to safety.

For a variety of reasons, Valdes' standing in the countryside was enhanced. Peasants rushed to join the *Guardia de Honor*. By September of 1898, Valdes could deploy more than 5,000 armed men in the Pangasinan, Tarlac, Nueva Ecija area. The movement became a major problem for the revolutionary government. While trying to deal with the American presence, Emilio Aguinaldo and his advisors received reports that areas loyal to the new republic were under attack from this new force. Military reinforcements had to be sent to bring some sense of order to the region. Sturtevant reads the events as taking on the "character of class warfare." (Sturtevant, 1976:104)

By February 1899, the *Guardia de Honor* was still a major force. The town of San Carlos, Pangasinan asked for government troops to protect its citizens from attacks of "those who call themselves the discontented or oppressed and Guards of Honor." (Sturtevant, 1976:105) However, the Philippine government was by that time engaged in a conflict with the Americans. When the Americans reached Pangasinan, they had to deal with the difficulties being caused by the *Agraviados*.

The Americans did not know what to make of these guerrillas. General Elwell Otis, the commander of American forces, regarded the religious aspect of the enemy as merely another example of "oriental perversity." (Sturtevant, 1976:106) He became convinced that the primary motivation was financial. When consulting with Manila's 'educated Filipinos,' he was warned of potential difficulties, but they had no answers.

Had the American commander assigned to deal with the *Agraviados*, General Arthur MacArthur, known the belief system of the movement, he would not have been any better off in terms of creating a solution. Cabaruan, the New Jerusalem, had a population of 25,000 in early 1901. Valdes, his principal advisor Gregorio Claveria, and their constant companion Maria de la Cruz, were worshipped respectively as Jesus Christ, the Holy Ghost, and the Virgin Mary. American forces occupied Cabaruan on March 3, 1901, capturing the religious trinity and the twelve lieutenants known as "the Savior's Apostles." On June 1, 1901, the trio was publicly hanged in Urdaneta, Pangasinan. (Sturtevant, 1976:111-113)

Sturtevant's conclusion regarding the *Guardia de Honor* reads as follows:

The transition to spiritual and political anarchy took more than a quarter of a century. When the process ended, the original sodality had undergone a metamorphosis: millennial ethics replaced Christian values; and violent rejection of all external authority supplanted passive acceptance of traditional control systems. (Sturtevant, 1976:96)

In seeking to understand the *Guardia de Honor* and other similar movements in Philippine history, two misconceptions must be corrected. The first is to view such movements as political or revolutionary. One finds this in Rey Ileto's intriguing *Pasyon and Revolution*, which interprets the religious tradition among Filipino peasants as having "latent meaning that can be revolutionary." (Ileto, 1997:10) This approach has been taken to much of Philippine history, particularly the Radical Tradition. Many accept the Spanish verdict that various movements were in fact seditious. But that is the Spanish point of view and need not be accepted as valid. Sedition is a political term, but the *Guardia de Honor* was not political. The Spaniards simply interpreted what they observed by what they knew. In the same way, radicalism in the nineteenth century is understood to be political.

The second misconception is found in Sturtevant's work, which views such movements as primarily religious. After all, the *Guardia de Honor* was a sodality—a cofradia, its members met for Masses, prayer meetings, etc. In the case of the *Guardia de Honor*, Sturtevant argues that it underwent a significant transformation, from a Christian movement to a millennial sect. David Sweet continues in this vein by suggesting that the religious character of the movement was "a strength rather than a weakness. It was its very other-worldliness which gave it organizational and revolutionary potential." (Sweet, 1970:155—cited in Ileto, 1977:29-30) Thus, Sweet and Ileto see such movements as religious on the surface, but revolutionary and thus, political, at its core.

The basis for regarding the movements as revolutionary or political is a belief that nineteenth century Filipinos had the same goals as other Filipinos: freedom, liberation. Ileto makes much of the word *kalayaan*, arguing that it is possible that *kalayaán* is quite distinct from *kalayáan*. That while the latter means freedom, the former points to something quite different. Ileto is correct that *kalayaan* did not mean freedom or independence prior to the rise of the Katipunan. Yet he still sees revolutionary meanings in the reading of the Pasyon pointing to liberation. So apart from *kalayaan*, Ileto sees liberation or freedom as the driving forces of these movements. But this is not the case. David Kelly in the first chapter of a newly released book entitled *Asian Freedoms*, refers to Orlando Patterson's view that "freedom was socially constructed, not discovered—for it was an invented value." (Kelly, 1998:8) Anthony Reid points out in his article in the same book, "Freedom as a key concept is either Western or it is modern." (Kelly, 1998:141) As such, it was not necessarily a value of those in the *Guardia de Honor*.

This does not mean that the members of the *Guardia de Honor* were happy or content with their situation; it is obvious that they were not. The movements can be viewed as attempts to improve their lives on a number of levels. There have been and will be responses on the part of the powerless; oftentimes defensive tactics. Does this mean then that they were primarily religious movements, using religious organizations as a means to respond to the difficulties in which they found themselves? The problem in asking this question is that the tendency to think of religion in the Western sense and particularly in terms of Catholicism, as indeed the *Guardia de Honor* was an organization, a sodality started within a Catholic context. But the movement changed. Why?

Melba Maggay poses the question: What happens when a religion of guilt confronts a religion of power? That is, what happens when Catholicism confronts or is confronted by a world view which focuses on power? In dealing with this contrast or confrontation, Maggay has noted several things, including the issues of guilt versus power. "It has been noted by many scholars that Christianity as it has developed theologically in the West has mostly centered on the complex of ideas surrounding sin and guilt." (Maggay, 1190:13) In the second part of her article, she points out that: "*Kasalanan* is a word made up by Spanish missionaries from the root word *sala*, which means 'mistake' or to miss the target. (Maggay, 1990:15) On the other hand, to the Filipino,

what counts most is access to the center of power that rules his life and the universe. His religious activity is focused on ways of opening oneself to the strength and curative potency of beneficial powers, whether they be in nature or in the spirit world. Prayers, devotions, sacrifices and ascetic practices such as denial of physical pleasure, fasting or self-mortification are mostly meant to increase potency. (Maggay, 1990;13)

Benedict Anderson's article *The Idea of Power in Javanese Culture* is invaluable in this area. Anderson lists four qualities in the Western concept of power: it is abstract; the sources of power are varied; the accumulation of power has no inherent limits; power is morally ambiguous. In contrast, in the Javanese view (and I would say that it is similar to the view held by those in the *Guardia de Honor*), the following four qualities are listed: power is concrete; power is homogeneous; the quantum of power in the universe is constant; power does not raise the issue of legitimacy. (Anderson, 1990:21-23) Thus, there is in fact a profound difference between the definitions and realizations of power.

Beyond the definitions of power are the different approaches to power. In the West, it is the exercise of power which is central, whereas in the Javanese system, it is the accumulation of power which is central. Thus, Maggay's comment above begins to explain the popularity of the sodalities, cofradias, or movements in the nineteenth and twentieth centuries, not as religious organizations per se, but as a means to accumulate power. The people in question sought to "harness these traditions" (Ileto, 1997:111) in pursuing their own view of the world, as they did for example with the legend of Bernardio Carpio. As Renato Constantino wrote:

We should remain constantly aware of the fact that as a result of colonial education we have hardly been exposed to the existence of a different world view—that of the masses of our people who have in their own way expressed their own ideas about the transformation of the world. (Constantino, 1997:11)

In the case of Julian Baltazar, the *anitero* leader of the *Guardia de Honor* and his wife, the "goddess," the issue is not in question. They and their followers were clearly in step with animism, the religion of power of that time. They simply subverted Catholic symbols and organization to express their world view.

Along the same lines, one should be careful not to assign twentieth-century meanings or implications to the language and terms used by these groups. *Damay* according to Ileto has the much older meaning of "participation in another's work," although inclusion is still a significant meaning of the word. (Ileto, 1997:51) But Ileto then sees the participation as being with the Jesus of the Pasyon, when in reality it is with the person of power, as one wishes to accumulate power. In the same way, the focus on *loob*, which is entirely appropriate, should then move not to *utang na loob* but to *lakas ng loob*. After all, *lakas ng loob* is the goal of the religion of power/animism. There is also the issue of *ginhawa*, which Ileto sees as reflecting prosperity, a general ease of life, relief from pain, sickness or difficulties. He shows that some believed that all of these were present before the Spaniards came and that all of these the various movements sought to regain. (Ileto, 1997:83) Using the metaphor of Adam and Eve in the Garden, then deceived by the serpent, the movements pointed to the damage done by the Spaniards. I would argue that rather than seeking a return to Eden, they were instead using a metaphor accessible to express what would happen when there was a shift of power in the universe. After all, the quantum of power is constant. If these movements were to gain power, the Spaniards and others would lose the power they had.

Then what connection should be made about the *Guardia de Honor* and the revolution? As much as one might try to avoid it, Western ideas did influence the leaders and those who guided the *Katipunan*. The earliest record of a call for independence in the

Philippines was in 1823. Led by Captain Andres Novales, a group of 800 Spaniards sought to overthrow the regime in power. Killing the interim governor-general, they shouted, "*Viva la Independencia.*" (Robles, 1969:36) There is no record that the *Katipuneros* were ever aware of that event. But the influence of the Propaganda Movement is undeniable. Composed of *ilustrado* sons in Spain, the Propaganda Movement reflected nineteenth-century European liberalism. Their writings did affect the *Katipunan.* But the secret rites and rituals which initiates were required to go through show a connection with other movements which thought in terms of *lakas ng loob.*

Great care should be taken in studying the radical tradition of the Philippines. Without question, some of the movements seem so remote from the present day, not only in terms of time, but also of world view. However, they are not any less a part of Philippine history. In remembering the Revolution, most find language, ideas, views which are readily accessible even one century later. This connection inclines the student of Philippine history to focus on such an event and to ignore what is unfamiliar and what perhaps even appears bizarre. At a recent conference on Philippine studies held at the University of California, Berkeley, a well-known Filipino writer in response to a paper given on millennarian sects in the Philippines, complained that such studies "only perpetuate the stupidity of the masses." I do not agree and I would respectfully submit that studying such movements is as important as the studying of the Philippine Revolution and other events which are more familiar. One must recognize that the individuals in the millennarian movements had as much claim to the title Filipino, *anak ng bayan,* as did any *Katipunero* or any other freedom-fighter in Philippine history.

NOTES

1. The historical information on the *Guardia de Honor* in this essay is drawn primarily and almost exclusively from chapter 5 of David Sturtevant's *Popular Uprisings in the Philippines: 1840-1940.* His research is based on Cipriano Pampliega's "Documento curioso sobre los guardias de honor de Pangasinan y otras cosas curiosas de los katipuneros," an unpublished manuscript in the Dominican Archives in Manila.

REFERENCES

Anderson, Benedict R. O'G. 1990. "The Idea of Power in Javanese Culture" in Anderson's *Language and Power: Exploring Political Cultures in Indonesia.* Ithaca: Cornell University Press.

Constantino, Renato. 1977. *Insight and Foresight.* Quezon City: Foundation for Nationalist Studies.

Ileto, Reynaldo Clemeña. 1997. *Pasyon and Revolution: Popular Movements in the Philippines, 1840-1910.* Manila: Ateneo de Manila University Press.

Kelly, David and Anthony Reid, eds. 1998. *Asian Freedoms: The Idea of Freedom in East and Southeast Asia.* Cambridge: Cambridge University Press.

Maggay, Melba. 1990 & 1991. "The Indigenous Religious Consciousness: Some Implications to Missions." *Patmos.* 6(2) and 7(1).

Robles, Eliodoro G. 1969. *The Philippines in the Nineteenth Century.* Quezon City: Malaya Books, Inc.

Sturtevant, David R. 1976. *Popular Uprisings in the Philippines* 1840-1940. Ithaca: Cornell University Press.

Sweet, David. 1970. "The Proto-Political Peasant Movement in the Spanish Philippines: The Cofradia de San Jose and the Tayabas Rebellion of 1841." *Asian Studies 8.*

POLITICAL CULTURE
AND IMPERIALISM:
THE PHILIPPINE EXPERIENCE [1]

Elizabeth A. Pastores-Palffy

By no means is this paper a regurgitation of Edward W. Said's *Culture and Imperialism* (1993)[2] because I consider my paper a pre-postcolonial interpretation of Philippine political culture. However, I found this title to capture the essence of this paper. This paper does not intend to provide a theoretical framework to analyze the interface of political culture and imperialism, but it is an attempt to see how the particular conditions of the Philippines and the particular type of imperialism the Americans had imposed on the colony resulted into a historical construct that is unique to the Philippine experience. This is more a theoretical discussion than the result of original research.

In this paper, I argue that: 1) American imperialism had profoundly influenced the formation of unique political cultures in the Philippines that were not necessarily intended by U.S. policy during 48 years of American colonial rule in the Philippines.

2) American imperialism had created a situation which polarized Filipinos further into two classes, the elites and the masses, leading to the development of diametrically-opposed political cultures: elite political culture and mass political culture.

So, here we speak of two political cultures that developed in response to American imperialism: one that embraced it and the other rejecting it. Both processes of collaboration and dissent have roots perhaps from the formation of sophisticated suprabaranganic or supreme datuship[3] and Islamic societies in the 15th century, and the 333 years of Spanish colonial domination of the country. But this division became more pronounced in the period under review.

Overview of Pre-American Philippine Political Cultures

Although not studied extensively, some anthropologists and historians have provided evidence about burgeoning polarized political cultures in Philippine societies at the Spanish contact. Other historians and anthropologists believe that because Philippine pre-colonial societies were democratic in nature, a more homogeneous type of political culture developed, one that was characterized by collective leadership and decision-making, cooperation, and support of physical prowess as a basis for power. I am sure there is truth to both claims. The first claim could have been true in the context of most advanced baranganic and Islamic societies, while the second could be true in less advanced baranganic societies. Overall, however, I can conclude from existing and established evidence[4] that the polarization of political cultures was not that clearly-defined during the precolonial times. We saw more of egalitarian societies where oppression and exploitation were not supported, where authority was seen as leadership, and political power as shared, not monopolized by a self-ordained chief.

It was against this background of political culture that Spanish colonialism was superimposed. The political culture that developed was one that polarized the colonizers and the colonized. At one end of the spectrum were natives who were powerless and were situated outside the grand colonial scheme. Although assigned a quasi-political position under the Spanish colonial regime, the Filipino *datu* (or Filipino chieftain) was an emasculated figure, a powerless errand man, and a symbolic leader. At the other end of the spectrum, we find the colonial Church and State which had always been perpetually at odds about the most appropriate methods of subjugating the native and about which of the two should reign supreme in the colony.

And so we visualize a society where the colonized population remained politically impotent and was gradually getting swallowed into the orbit of the plaza complex culture. We clearly see a dominant-dominated dichotomy between colonizer and colonized within the microcosm of the *pueblo* (or town). Because of this structure, the native Filipino, otherwise known as *Indio* had become more accepting of colonial authority and passive about his destiny. The Church had definitely accomplished its task of emasculating the *Indio*. We know from history, however, that this "passive reaction" did not remain the same. Sporadic revolts erupted in various parts of the country. Irrespective of revolutionary responses, however, the Spanish colonial regime had created a climate where Filipinos distrusted authority, where Filipinos became impotent politically and economically, where *Indio* political culture had no identity of its own. The *Indio* was practically relegated to the background, voiceless and powerless. Three centuries of silence characterized Philippine political culture under Spanish rule, three crucial centuries that stunted the development of a homegrown political system whose identity was amorphous. Philippine political culture under the Spanish colonial regime, therefore, was one that did not have a local or native identity, one that emphasized the power relations between the colonizer and the colonized, one that prevented natives from participating in the political process, and one that rendered them merely reactive, not proactive to the political life of the colony.

Filipino intellectuals who became politically conscious challenged this structure in the 19th century. These Filipino intellectuals were collectively known as *ilustrados* whose ancestry was traced back to Spanish and Chinese roots. It was this group that benefited from the impact of liberalism. Being wealthy, *ilustrado* families sent their children to study at reputable institutions in Manila and in Spain. Exposed to liberal ideas and a genuine commitment to the struggle for "Filipino" participation in "colonial government," the *ilustrados* stirred the minds and hearts of others who felt that it was time to have the voice of the Filipino heard in the political arena. Initial expressions of protest came in the form of "nationalist writings." Others expressed it in art form. All these tools of protest might have reached only the "literate" sector of society but it was sufficient to awaken the national consciousness of a significant sector of the population. Even Andres Bonifacio, the revolutionary leader of the masses, derived inspiration from the writings and experience of Jose Rizal, the recognized leader of the *ilustrado* nationalists. However, the masses and the *ilustrados* digressed in their goals and methods of protest. The *ilustrados* asserted political participation within the existing colonial framework while the masses struggled for complete independence from colonial rule. *Ilustrados* advocated only a peaceful approach to attain their goals. The masses believed that only a revolutionary struggle would pave their way to genuine participation in the political process. So, although we see the *ilustrados* and the masses sharing nationalist sentiments, the differences as stated manifested themselves towards the end of the Revolution and they persisted throughout the next colonial period in Philippine history.

A brief transition period between Spanish colonialism and American imperialism afforded the Filipinos an opportunity to experiment on self-government, albeit a revolutionary government in exile. Although a new political structure had been laid out as mandated by the so-called Malolos constitution, this "experimental government" was rife with conflicts. Even before it could get off the ground, this transitional government was compromised by a secret agreement between the Spaniards and Americans to turn over the Philippines to the Americans at the tune of $20 million.[5] Once again, the Filipinos found themselves helpless under a new colonial regime.

Intent of American Colonial Policy and Filipino Response

Codified policy indicated that the native Filipinos were to be trained toward self-government. It indicated further that Filipinos were to adopt the principles of democracy via a public school system that would be accessible to all. The stage was set to "create the Philippines in America's own image." All these were planned without regard to the idiosyncracies of Philippine political life and behavior, and lack of recognition for the potential of Filipinos to run their own affairs as proven historically by the short-lived Malolos Congress. All these, were done also without regard to the Filipinos' own concept of democracy and self-government. Democracy in Philippine context was inseparable to freedom and independence. And self-government meant that Filipinos would have decision-making powers. Self-government within the context of American colonial policy did not extend those powers to them. Some semblance of power may be evident, but it remained superficial. The intent of imperialism was not to offer political power to the colonized. Political decisions solely resided in the hands of the US Congress and the US President. American governor-generals and later, the US High Commissioners assigned to oversee the Philippine colony, assured the authorities that American policy was maintained and executed with minimum resistance.

Power was superimposed and the Filipinos were silenced. What choice could Filipinos have under colonial domination? The elites or former *ilustrados* were left only with two options: cooptation or collaboration. Some revolutionary intellectuals asserted their voices through "seditious writings and plays." The masses on the other hand were beginning to build up their own powerbase. Although not intended by American colonial policy, colonial policy itself had perpetuated the rift between the masses and the elites. For instance, property requirements were necessary to run for public office, automatically excluding the masses from participating in the "legitimate" political processes. Where the elites opted to be coopted or to collaborate, the masses opted for separation from colonial power. Let me qualify that statement by saying that a few of the elites supported the cause of the masses, while not all of the masses supported the idea of separation. Here we see a unique situation of interplay between colonizers and elites on one hand, and elites and the masses on the other. Where the colonized, whether elites or masses, were completely separated from the colonizer under the Spanish colonial regime, the Filipino elites under the American colonial regime were extended some semblance of "political participation" within a colonial structure. This phenomenon created a situation where the rift between the elites and the masses would intensify. During the Spanish period the elites and the masses were jointly oppressed by colonization. Both were placed totally outside of the Spanish political framework. When opportunity presented itself for "Filipino participation" in politics (i.e., via the Filipino revolutionary government), class differences tore up a potentially unified political structure. With cooptation of elites or their collaboration with the American colonial regime, the differences became more pronounced.

Profile of Philippine Political Culture Under American Rule

Under American rule, Philippine political culture was generally characterized by: 1. dominant-dominated power relationships (i.e., colonizer versus colonized and political elite versus masses); 2. development of a non-indigenous political system patterned after the American model (two-house Congress: upper house, lower house, two-party system, presidential system); 3. the *compadrazco* system[6] which somehow legitimized or sanctioned corruption in politics; 4. development of a mass political powerbase which challenged the stability of American and Filipino elite partnership, leading up to the formation of diametrically-opposed political cultures: one created in America's own image and the other resisting this image; and,
5. the development of the Filipino as an incomplete political being as a result of centuries of being politically impotent under colonial regimes.

Dominant-Dominated Power Relationships

The political structure under American colonial rule was characterized by dominant-dominated power relationships, that is, colonizer versus colonized and political elite versus masses. A group of American scholars[7] argue that "American style imperialism" was unique in the sense that the colonized "shared" in the governance of the colony. These scholars argue further that Filipinos were trained by the American colonizers for "self-government." These claims have since been questioned by other scholars in the field (mostly Filipino scholars) who hold the view that so-called shared governance and "self-government" were tools of domination rather than genuine attempts to include Filipinos in the political process. They warned that this particular type of imperialism could lead others to believe that American imperialism was benevolent imperialism in the sense that some Filipinos were offered "political offices" through colonial sponsorship. They argued that there is no such thing as "benevolent imperialism," that the motive for assigning Filipinos to certain offices was just a strategy to mitigate resistance and to coopt supporters, as well as provide a semblance of Filipino political participation under a colonial political structure. They also contended that a record of discussions in Washington revealed that "willing" Filipinos would be utilized to assist in carrying out American policy because it would be a cost-effective measure in the operations of the colony. Some Filipinos (mostly Filipino elites) certainly collaborated voluntarily with the new colonial regime. According to Cruz,[8] Filipinos collaborated at the beginning of American colonial rule in the hope of gaining support for their struggle against the Spaniards while others did it for self-preservation.

A larger picture shows that whatever happened (cooptation, collaboration, self-government and so on) it was a fact that Filipino politicians did not really have an effective voice in this colonial regime. They were there to serve as pawns against real or imagined enemies of the colonial government, as well as, to help carry out the goals of American imperialism.

Clearly, collaboration and cooptation served as effective instruments of dividing and ruling the population. These actions only created a wider gap between the elite and the masses in the political as well as the economic realm. To run for even the smallest public office, a candidate must own property. It was common to see landlords or landlord-sponsored candidates running for elections in the period under review. In this situation, the masses were excluded entirely from the "legitimate" political processes.

From the surface it seemed like American style imperialism was indeed unique in the sense that Filipinos were encouraged to participate in the political process. What was glossed over, however, was the fact that political participation was extremely limited by property requirements and that real decision-making power did not really reside in Filipino hands, in effect failing to fully-develop Filipinos as mature politicians. More about this issue in a later section of the paper.

Development of a Non-Indigenous Political System Patterned after the American Model

One striking feature of Philippine political culture under American rule was the eventual transfer of American political practices into Philippine soil. There was no wholesale transfer, but significant enough for the Philippines to earn the appellation, "created in its own (American) image." Of all countries in Asia, only the Philippines was be "profoundly" influenced by the American political system. Some inherited political institutions and practices that remain evident today include: political vocabulary, electoral practices, system of party government, jurisprudence, doctrines of constitutionalism, and theories of administrative management.[9]

The end result of this "borrowed political system" was the formation of a cadre of semi-politicians (semi in the sense of half-developed) that mouthed the American principles of democracy and that ascertained these political institutions and practices were in place. Obviously, it also resulted into the adoption of political practices that were not exactly compatible or suitable to Philippine conditions and needs, as well as to Filipino temperament. Indeed, the American grand design to "subjugate peoples with a difference" proved to be a success at least in the eyes of those who were ignorant of the context in which it happened.

It is claimed by many historians that remnants of indigenous politics remained at the lowest level of government, i.e., at the municipal government level. I argue, however, that even that remained superficially indigenous. Indigenous concepts or terminologies might have been adopted but the essence of the baranganic tradition was no longer there. However, would the baranganic system have been an appropriate structure for Filipinos under changed conditions? One argument was that profound changes have occurred through centuries of subjugation that indigenous political systems were no longer relevant to the existing political structure. The counter-argument was that indigenous systems could be far more responsive to the needs of the people than an entirely foreign system because the former were deeply-rooted in tradition and were structured in response to the people's needs and idiosyncracies. In reality, however, the Filipinos were not really free to design their own political destinies. So, whether Filipinos thought the system was appropriate or not, did not really matter to the colonial regime. The American model was up for grabs (none other was available to choose from) and some Filipinos had no other recourse but to adopt that model.

We see therefore the gradual inroad of American-style politics in the Philippines. Nurtured both by powerholders in Washington and the Filipino elite (who stood to gain from this set-up), the Americanized political system dominated the Philippine political scene for many years to come. No one bothered to evaluate its compatibility or incompatibility with Philippine political tradition. The end result was alienation on the part of the Filipino masses from political institutions and practices that were entirely foreign to their own experience. I have to add, however, that some Filipinos adapted to it quite well.

The *Compadrazco* System in Colonial Context

One interesting feature of Philippine political culture in the period under review was the application of the *compadrazco*[10] concept to Philippine politics. This concept defined the relationship between the United States and the Philippines during the American colonial period, as well as the relationship of the Filipino elite with each other and with the masses.

In terms of US-Philippine relations, Norman Owen[11] (an American Filipinist) speaks about accommodations and compromises between American colonial administrators and Filipino leaders. By *compadre* colonialism, he meant that local leaders and American colonizers have joined together to exercise power over the Philippine colony. He traced the origin of this *compadre* concept to *ilustrado*-Spanish collusion in the 19th century. In his article, he stated that Filipino *ilustrados* had a tendency to gravitate towards sources of power[12] and that this tendency was carried over to the American period with the Americans now taking the place of the Spaniards.

Literally, a *compadre* (or loosely translated as co-parent) is a person who is given authority to serve as guardian of a child. He or she is not necessarily related to the child by blood but he or she serves the function of a secondary parent. *Compadrazco* therefore means extension of family relations beyond blood kinship. The Catholic Church with baptismal, confirmation, and wedding rituals institutionalized the practice. At a macro level, the Filipino elite represented the parent, the American colonial administrators the co-parent or *compadre,* and the Filipino people the child. In reality, however, the co-parent or the adoptive parent was the more powerful figure in this partnership, in effect serving the role of parent more than co-parent. So, there might have been some truth to Owen's allegation that Filipino *ilustrados* tended to gravitate towards sources of power, but it might be more accurate to say that colonialism created the environment that made this special partnership possible. Furthermore, the relationship was unequal. I therefore question the validity of the *compadrazco* concept to explain the "equal partnership in crime" theory. To a certain extent, it was true that the Filipino elite participated in colonial administration, but I would view this more as part of the grand design of America to colonize the Philippines as efficiently and as effectively as possible. The *compadrazco* system obviously served certain purposes of American colonialism. For one, it was a way to hide the realities of a dominant-dominated relationship as it gave a semblance of equal partnership. Knowing that it was a favorable trait for the Filipinos, American colonizers had used it as a tool to ease the tensions between themselves and the local rulers as well as win the confidence of the masses. In general, it was a way to prove that a country can be colonized with a difference, supporting the "theory of benevolent American imperialism" that some scholars have promoted .[13]

The concept is applied quite differently in terms of relationships among the Filipino political elite and the elite with other members of society. We could say that it promoted nepotism in politics as well as unequivocal support of one *compadre* politician to another. No matter how minimal their participation in the political affairs of the colony, the *compadre* politicians mutually reinforced each other. This practice encouraged corruption during elections and while the politician was in office. *Compadre* relationship connoted asking and granting favors to a *"compadre"* blindly. This practice may not have been that prevalent in the period under review but the preponderance of the practice after independence clearly had its roots during the colonial times.

The Development of a Mass Political Powerbase

Many scholars gloss over the politics of the masses when discussing Philippine political culture under American rule. The role of the elite has been overemphasized by most scholars, failing in effect to provide a comprehensive picture of Philippine political culture in the period under review. The political culture of the masses was characterized as amorphous, disorganized, and unstructured, in contrast to that of the Filipino elite. The masses rejected the presence of a foreign power in the country and resented what they view as partnership between this foreign power and the Filipino political elite. They believed that this partnership was inimical to the interests of the Filipino people.

This new mass powerbase had its roots mostly from farmer and labor interests. According to Corpuz,[14] "their party organizations have been pushed to the fringes of the party system by the established parties, thus their interests have had no direct organized influence on national electoral decisions." As a result, they were forced to engage in so-called "illegitimate" political activities to fight for their cause.

In the early years of American rule, various types of mass-based groups not necessarily peasant and labor-based have emerged to demonstrate their defiance to authority. They included the so-called seditious writers, and what Sturtevant in his book *Popular Uprising in the Philippines, 1840-1940,* called *ladrones, ladrones politicos,* and *ladrones fanaticos.*[15] Indeed, those who defied authority were branded as bandits or outlaws. The movements led by former revolutionaries such as Macario Sakay, Artemio Ricarte, "Dimas-Alang," and "Makabuhay" stood out.[16] In 1903, Macario Sakay proclaimed himself the Supreme President of the Filipino Republic with the Rizal-Cavite-Laguna-Batangas nucleus as his territory. Later on, he was hanged for treason but his movement indicated the rising fervor of the masses to assert their political voice. It also signified their rising discontent against American rule.

Less politicized yet another attempt at establishing a political powerbase was by leaders of millenarian or revitalization movements or what Sturtevant referred to in his book as *ladrones fanaticos*.[17] Although marginalized, their presence and activities throughout the American regime have certainly annoyed the American authorities. They created a political subculture that appeared to be organized, yet not powerful or politicized enough to challenge the existing order.

The seditious writers and playwrights found themselves in a similar situation. They were powerless to defend themselves against a mighty political machinery. Their works had often been slapped with the Sedition Law crippling any attempt on their part to reach a wider audience. As a result, their voice reached only a limited audience.

The peasant and labor-based organizations caused the most concern among American officials. These organizations proved to be politically potent and posed the greatest potential threat to the colonial order: the Sakdal movement, the *Partido Obrero de Filipinas,* and the Communist Party of the Philippines, to name only a few. Evangelista, Ponce, and Bognot formed the *Partido Obrero de Filipinas* in 1924 as a counterpoise to the Nacionalista Party. The program of this labor group became the basis for the program of the Communist Party of the Philippines. Labor congresses they sponsored had brought together labor and peasant groups throughout the nation. The *Partido* gave rise to a more broad-based organization (now comprising both peasant and labor groups) called *Congreso Obrero de Filipinas,* otherwise known as *Katipunan ng mga Anak-Pawis ng Pilipinas* (or K.A.P.).[18]

Sakdalism[19] constituted another threat to the existence of American colonialism in the Philippines. The name of the group came from *Sakdal*, a newspaper founded by Benigno Ramos in 1930. It became the mouthpiece by which peasants have expressed their grievances. It also served as the nucleus from which the *Sakdal* Party was formed which declared participation in the 1934 general election. Although the Party had its ups and downs, it attracted a large following of discontented peasants.[20] In 1935, *Sakdal* leaders launched barrio campaigns to rally the people to boycott the plebiscite for the Commonwealth Constitution. When threatened with arrest by government officials, 150 peasants armed with *bolos* marched to the municipal building of San Ildefonso, Bulacan, hauled down the American and Philippine flags and raised the red *Sakdal* flag. Other uprisings ensued in provinces around Manila. It was believed that about 60,000 *Sakdalistas* were involved in the revolt. Due to the absence of a leader (Ramos was in Japan at that time), and the firepower of the government, the revolts were easily quelled. Despite the failure of the movement, the K.A.P. and *Sakdal* incidents proved to the ruling government that the Filipino peasants and laborers were capable of organizing a large group that could threaten the stability of the colonial regime.[21] Although the legal life of the Communist Party of the Philippines was nipped in the bud from its inception in 1930, its influence continued to be felt in various peasant and workers' organizations. Before it was declared illegal by the Supreme Court on October 26, 1932, it organized a meeting of unions in Manila, supported labor strikes and peasant actions. In a show of solidarity, about 10,000 workers marched in the funeral of Antonio Ora, a Communist leader, who died mysteriously in an automobile accident. Red flags and placards screamed anti-imperialist slogans.[22] Although weakened and quelled eventually, these movements had certainly posed a threat to the established order.

Unfortunately for the masses, all the mass-based groups were not linked to each other, by virtue of ideological differences. A form of communication or linkage among them was evident but it did not get to a point where all the organizations would come together under one umbrella.

The point of this paper is to show that a mass political powerbase was being formed alongside elite political structures. These mass organizations might have remained in the fringes, but their significance to the understanding of Philippine political culture under a colonial regime cannot be underemphasized considering the magnitude of their political activities.

So, while collaboration and cooptation defined the political elite's relationship with colonial power, rejection and resistance defined that of the masses. These mass movements developed a political culture that had indigenous character and that developed outside of the "legitimate" political environment. Whether called alternative or political subculture, the mass political organizations had developed a political culture independently but parallel to mainstream or elite political culture. Most of these organizations were formed in reaction to the growing strength of elite political organizations. This contradiction became a constant feature of Philippine politics after independence.

Filipino Political Elites Becoming Politically Impotent

In any colonial structure, there is hardly a chance for the colonized to fully develop their potential as career politicians. In Philippine context, the precolonial local rulers were too far removed from history to serve as role models for the Filipino "politician." Besides, the objective conditions have changed significantly to make the precolonial model obsolete. The revolutionary government was too short-lived for rising politicians to consider as a model government to emulate. Its transitory character made it even more difficult for the Filipino politicians of the American period to evaluate its relevance to conditions at that time, thus the revolutionary fathers who were "rookie" politicians themselves could not be seen as their political mentors; not to speak of ideological differences between themselves and their predecessors. The revolutionary fathers aimed at complete separation from colonizers, while the Filipino political elite during the American period worked towards assimilation within the colonial framework.

Although some semblance of political freedom existed under American colonial rule, this freedom remained limited. There was really no opportunity for Filipino politicians to explore politics on their own because their actions were dictated by colonial policy. So we see the development of a half-baked politician, an imitator politician if you will, who became politically inutile because he could not really have an effective voice in a colonial regime. The most immediate role model was the American model which was adopted without regard to the idiosyncracies and realities of Philippine political life. In short, a mismatch between Filipino politicians and the cultural context in which they operated would ensue, resulting to alienation of the Filipino masses from their own leaders.

This phenomenon was best exemplified by the track records of the "big political triumvirates" in Philippine politics in the period under review, namely: Osmeña, Quezon, and Roxas. Although well-meaning and nationalistic in their stance, the truth was, they were all sitting in a political ivory tower, nonchalant about the conditions of the people they served or unable to become more responsive to their needs, much less identify with their causes. After all, they were placed in an ambivalent situation where they served two entities, which had conflicting goals: nationalism and independence for the Filipino people and imperialism for the American colonial rulers. They talked about nationalism yet mouthed the colonial will on the Filipino people. That is why I call them half-baked politicians in the sense that they could not be fully-independent to practice politics and make decisions on their own in their own land.

Summary and Conclusion

So, we see a historical construct that is unique to the Philippine experience. American style imperialism has certainly claimed the Philippines to be its show window of democracy in Asia. It also tried to prove to the world that a colony could certainly be ruled with a difference. Many scholars ask, where in the world could you find imperialist rulers sharing governance with the colonized and train them for self-government? Other scholars believe that in the over-all scheme of things, governance was not truly shared and Filipino politicians were not really prepared for self-government. At best, Filipino politicians got exposed to American political culture, adopted some of its characteristics, and functioned with them in a colonial setting. At worst, it denied Filipino politicians the right to full political maturation. In short, American colonial rule only delayed the full development of the Filipino elite as a politician.

Concurrent with this development was the growth of a political culture that had indigenous character and grew outside of the "legitimate political structure." This political culture developed by the masses generated a culture of protest against the existing colonial order. The masses represented various groups whose character, methods of protest, ideologies, and organizations differed, but whose common goal was rejection of foreign rule.

Further polarization between the masses and the elite ensued: one operating within legitimate bounds and the other outside of those bounds. This resulted into the development of diametrically opposed political cultures: elite political culture and mass political culture—one at the upper end of the political spectrum, the other at the lower end. At no time in the history of the country prior to the postwar period had this division become more pronounced. These political cultures developed independently from each other and occasionally clashed against each other. Intentional or not, the colonial environment certainly fostered greater polarization between these two cultures which somehow dictated the directions Philippine politics had taken after independence from the United States and beyond.

NOTES

1. Paper originally presented at the 1995 Annual meeting of the American Historical Association (Pacific Coast Branch), 4-7 August 1995 at the Intercontinental Hotel, Maui, Hawaii.

2. Edward W. Said, *Culture and Imperialism*, New York, Knopf, 1993

3. A term used in Ferdinand Marcos, *Tadhana Outline: The History of the Filipino People*, Manila: Media Production Center, 1975.

4. See Teodoro Agoncillo and Milagros Guerrero, *History of the Filipino People*, Fifth Edition, Quezon City: R.P. Garcia Publishing Co., 1977: and, Renato Constantino, *The Philippines: A Past Revisited*, Quezon City, Tala Publishing Services, 1975.

5. Agoncillo, p.241.

6. *Compadre Colonialism: Studies on the Philippines Under American Rule*, Edited by Norman Owen. Michigan Papers on South and

Southeast Asia (No. 3, 1971). Michigan: University of Michigan Center for South and Southeast Asian Studies, 1971, p.1. Hereafter cited as Owen.

7. These historians include Onorato. Among his works showing evidence of this view is: Michael Ornorato, *A Brief Review of American Interest in Philippine Development and Other Essays.* Revised Edition, Manila: MCS Enterprises, Inc., 1972.

8. Romeo Cruz, *America's Colonial Desk in the Philippines: 1898-1934*, Ph.D. Dissertation in History, University of California at Berkeley, 1972.

9. Onofre D. Corpus, *The Philippines.* New Jersey: Prentice-Hall, Inc., 1965 p. 69.

10. *Compadrazco* is a type of relationship that extended family relationships to the godparents *compadres* of one's child. This system was institutionalized by the Catholic Church via the sacraments of baptism, confirmation, and matrimony.

11. Owen p. 1.

12. *Ibid.*, p. 2.

13. These historians include Brands and Blount, among others. See James J. Blounts's *The American Occupation of the Philippines, 1898-1912,* New York, 1912; and H.W. Brands, *Bound to Empire: The United States and the Philippines*, New York: Oxford University Press, 1992.

14. Corpus, p. 107.

15. David R. Sturtevant, *Popular Uprisings in the Philippines, 1840-1940.* Ithaca: Cornell University Press, 1976, p. 119.

16. Bonifacio Salamanca, *The Filipino Reaction to American Rule, 1901-*

1913, Quezon City, Philippines: New Day Publishers, 1984, p. 155.

17. Sturtevant, p. 119.

18. Constantino, pp. 360-361.

19. Sturtevant, p. 218-222

20. *Ibid.*

21. Constantino, pp. 367-370

22. *Ibid*, pp. 361-362.

REFERENCES

Agoncillo, Teodoro. 1974. *Filipino Nationalism, 1872-1970*. Quezon City: R.P. Garcia Publishing Co.

Agoncillo, Teodoro and Milagros C. Guerrero. 1977. *History of the Filipino People*. Quezon City: R.P. Garcia Publishing Co.

Blount, James. *1912 The American Occupation of the Philippines, 1898-1912*. New York .

Brands, H.W. 1992. *Bound to Empire: The United states and the Philippines*. New York: Oxford University Press.

Chilton, Stephen. 1991. *Grounding Political Development*. Boulder: Lynne Rienner Publishers.

Constantino, Renato. 1975. *The Philippines: A Past Revisited*. Quezon City: Tala Publishing Services.

Corpuz, Onofre. 1965. *The Philippines*. New Jersey: Prentice Hall.

Cranson, Maurice, and Lea Campos Boralevi, eds. 1988, *Culture and Politics*. Berlin: Walter de Gruyter.

Cruz, Romeo. 1972. *America's Colonial Desk in the Philippines:1898-1934*. Ph.D. Dissertation in History. University of California at Berkeley.

De la Costa, H. 1965. *Readings in Philippine History*. Manila: Bookmark.

Diamond, Larry, ed. 1993. *Political Culture and Democracy in Developing Countries*. Boulder: Lynne Rienner Publishers.

Marcos, Ferdinand. 1975. *Tadhana Outline: History of the Filipino People*. Manila: Media Production Center.

May, Glenn. 1980. *Social Engineering in the Philippines: The Aim, Execution, and Impact of American Colonial Policy*. Westport, Connecticut: Greenwood Press.

Owen, Norman, ed. 1971. *Compadre Colonialism: Studies on the Philippines Under American Rule*. Michigan Papers on South and Southeast Asia (No. 3). Michigan: The University of Michigan Center for South and Southeast Asian Studies.

Pomeroy, William. 1970. *American Neocolonialism: Its Emergence in the Philippine and Asia*. New York: International Publishers.

Said, Edward. 1993. *Culture and Imperialism*. New York: Knopf.

Salamanca, Bonifacio. 1984. *The Filipino Reaction to American Rule, 1901-1913*. Quezon City: New Day Publishers.

Schirmer, Daniel, and Stephen Rosskamm, Shalom, eds. 1987. *The Philippines Reader: A History of Colonialism, Neocolonialism, Dictatorship, and Resistance* Boston: South End Press.

Sturtevant, David R. 1976. *Popular Uprisings in the Philippines, 1840-1940*. Ithaca: Cornell University Press.

Tan, Samuel K. 1987. *A History of the Philippines.* Quezon City: University of the Philippines, Department of History.

Veneracion, Jaime. 1987. *Agos ng Dugong Kayumanggi.* Quezon City: Education Forum.

Wilson, Richard. 1992. *Compliance Ideologies: Rethinking Political Culture.* Cambridge: Cambridge University Press.

CHRISTIANITY
IN THE PHILIPPINES:
SOME REFLECTIONS ON
A SPANISH LEGACY

Santiago Sia

A centennial celebration is always a time for stock-taking. The passage of a hundred years must surely provoke some thoughts about the past in one form or another. In some cases, this stock-taking could involve the mere recounting of incidents which occurred during that period. In other cases, it will take the shape of objectively analyzing any developments which may or may not have taken place in those years. In most instances, however, an appropriate way to mark such an important event is to reflect on its significance and to explore its meaning for those who have been and will be affected by it.[1] Admittedly such an undertaking will inevitably result in an expression of a point of view and thus of a more subjective interpretation of what has happened. It is also likely that such reflections are formed by one's particular interests and concerns. Nevertheless, it is in such exchange of points of view on the significance of the past—no matter how subjective and specific these may be—that we can discover its many dimensions which otherwise will remain hidden if one merely recounted or analyzed what has happened. Moreover, it is when we thoughtfully review the past that we can sometimes appreciate the present and even draw lessons for the future.

This centennial celebration is no exception. And in this context it is more than appropriate that we turn our attention to Christianity in the Philippines. A hundred years ago, the Philippines gained its freedom from Spanish rule. Whatever one may think of Spain's dominance in our country for three centuries, we cannot deny that a strong legacy it left behind is the Catholic Christian religion[2]. Again, we may entertain different and even conflicting assessments of that legacy; but we will have to accept that it has influenced—rightly or wrongly, superficially or deeply—the vast majority of our people. During this centennial celebration, it seems to be especially timely, therefore, to offer some reflections on what Spain has left behind in our country.

In this essay, I do not intend to assess the kind of Christianity that Spain bequeathed to the Philippines, much less do I want to provide some kind of commentary on the way Christianity, since its introduction by the Spanish friars, has made a mark on the Filipino way of life.[3] Instead, I wish to share a reflective interpretation of the Christian message, several years after those who had brought it to our country had finally departed. In other words, this essay concerns itself with a certain understanding of that legacy as it applies to our country and to our people today. I believe that this venture is more in keeping with the theme of this volume of essays. In these reflections, I focus initially on a specific event, namely EDSA, because I see it as illustrating a particular development in the way Christianity in the Philippines has come to be understood by many of us.[4] It should not, however, be assumed that I am affirming that this dramatic moment in the country's recent history is entirely what Philippine Christianity is all about or that the future of Christianity is dependent on the success or failure of what EDSA had set out to achieve. Rather, the significance of EDSA, as far as this particular understanding of Philippine Christianity is concerned, is that it made explicit what I believe had already been present, although in different forms and with some sporadic bursts, in its earlier history.[5]

EDSA as Symbol

Let us first of all re-live what took place a few years ago in the Philippines and reflect on its significance in the context of the topic of this essay.

In February 1986 the world's attention seemed to have focused on the Philippines—at least for a few days. Suddenly the political life of that country was of terrific interest to the world's media. Through news coverage, particularly by television, many became aware of what was happening in Manila. There were even some gripping moments. As one watched the news, one started to follow the events and to await developments: what is happening? who are the main characters? how will it end? The drama was unfolding at a fast pace.

That event was the toppling down of Ferdinand Marcos, who held power in the Philippines for over twenty years.[6] It was a most unexpected occurrence. The way it turned out was just as much of a surprise. Television pictures showed ordinary people, students, professionals, nuns and clergy, stopping the military—not with guns but by songs and prayers! The Catholic leader of the Philippines, Cardinal Sin, had publicly urged the people to take action! It seemed so unreal—except for the fact that Marcos was finally forced to step down and leave the country. It was billed a great victory for "people power."

To many that event lasted a few days. But to those who had experienced the build-up to that moment, it represented years of struggle and innumerable attempts to change the political structure of the country. It would not have occurred without the active participation of the main characters—the Filipino people. It was after all "by the people and about the people." Some would interpret that event as a political maneuver. But there was more to it: to insiders it was action that was inspired by a commitment for social justice among the poor. Unless one takes serious account of that point, one would indeed brush off that event as another interference by the churches in politics. On the other hand, if one is prepared to see more closely, one will understand why—at least to some of us—that turning point in the political life of the Philippines is what Christianity has come to mean in that country. Despite the fact that it occurred more than a decade ago and no matter what the later developments have been, that event symbolizes and illustrates the issues and challenges that Filipino Christians are faced with today.

EDSA and Philippine Christianity

Christianity came to the Philippines with the arrival of the Spaniards in 1521. Their presence in the country, lasting for more than three centuries, ensured that Catholic Christianity would obviously affect the Filipino people and their way of life. Although its development has been closely linked with Western culture and Western politics, some attempts were made, even during Spanish times, to integrate Christianity with the lives and cultures of the Filipino people. The fact that it has continued to be the main religion of the country must somehow be a testimony to some success in the integration process. It would be naive, of course, to overlook some of the less acceptable reasons why many Filipinos continue to be Christians. Some would even object to the "Christianity" of some Filipinos and, therefore, would question any claim to a successful integration. Nonetheless, the fact is that the Philippines remains a predominantly Christian nation in Asia. Why this is so is another matter, a much more complex one.

In taking the EDSA event (which has become the name given to that February event since it took place at Epifanio de los Santos Avenue) as my starting point for reflecting on Christianity in the Philippines, I am focusing on a particular understanding of Christianity in the Philippines rather than on the reasons for Filipino Christianity. Aside from the fact that a sociological analysis required by the latter point is beyond my competence, I also believe that the main challenge that we are faced with in the Philippines in our time is to show how the Christian message, which we have been hearing for more than four centuries now, can address the problems we are experiencing in the Philippine context. I interpret that message to mean that Philippine Christianity today is about the plight of the Filipino people: about being empowered so that they can work towards their liberation. There is, of course, nothing distinctive about saying that Christianity is about the liberation of people since clearly it has always been so although now and then other considerations have been given the upper-hand. But there is something specific in the way this message applies to the Filipino people. This is not because we have a unique set of problems nor because our background is different. It is not even because our history and politics set us apart from our Asian neighbors. Instead it is all of these combined.

Filipinos continually use the phrase: "That is very Filipino" and other Filipinos would instinctively understand what is meant. EDSA was a very Filipino way of expressing our understanding of Christianity in the Philippines. Just as that event was mainly about people who wanted to take control of their lives, so is the meaning of Christianity to many Filipinos. Filipino Christianity is largely about the Filipino people. Part of our history and a significant feature of our identity are closely linked to Christianity.

Let me explain. EDSA was about life, about wanting to be allowed to live more fully as human beings. It was an action by people who had been struggling amidst oppression, poverty and exploitation. *"Tama na"* (enough) was a cry coming out of the crowd. *"Mabuhay ang Pilipino!"* (roughly, Let Filipinos live). Similarly, we interpret the Christian message as one that will enable us to live the fullness of life. We have had enough of the downside of life. In the context of the Philippines that message is about being liberated from every type of oppression which hinders the full development of human life. EDSA was not just about politics or economics. It was about human existence. It was about the experience of millions of Filipinos who were rightfully clamoring for a more human kind of existence. Finally, EDSA gave us a glimmer of hope. We had struggled, we had been conscientized, we had dialogued—now we wanted a better future.

I am sure many Filipinos present at that event did not have a clear idea of what was ahead—to claim otherwise would be to impose a certain interpretation of their expectations. But I doubt whether that really mattered. Filipinos are fond of saying *"Bahala na"* (roughly, let it take care of itself or leave it to Bathala or God). The unclarity of the future does not deter Filipinos from seeking a change in their situation. Instead, the EDSA event was going to give them some reason to hope, and that was what really counted.

In the same way, Christianity for us is a message of hope. But it should be a message of hope that is rooted in reality. Christianity should not alienate us from the fact that we are human beings. It should uplift our humanity, not despise it. It should seek to transform this world that we inhabit, not replace it. At the same time, however, we cannot focus exclusively on the present reality and ignore the future. We need to be reminded that there is a future. The future being what it is, we need to be open and even trusting. What this amounts to is that, in asking us to put our hope in the future, Christianity wants us to work for the future even as we concern ourselves with the present. I think that this is a great challenge to Philippine Christianity, particularly in our time. The phrase *"bahala na"* can be a cloak for laziness (as indeed it often is, unfortunately); thus, we need to show in Christian terms what hoping in and trusting in the future really means and the responsibilities it entails.

The Christian Message for the Philippines Today:
An Interpretation

Let me now move away from what EDSA symbolized and illustrated to focusing more closely on what has already been stated briefly: namely, that Christianity in the Philippines is about our people, our life and our hope. In making this claim, I am maintaining that the Christian message is in a sense about our past since we are who we are because of our history. It is also a reference to our present insofar as what we are concerned with is the kind of life our people live today. Furthermore, it has a bearing on our future inasmuch as we need to be able to hope for a better tomorrow. All these really mean the one thing: the Christian message for the Philippines today means empowering the Filipino people.

Let me say something about each of these points. Because of our history and geographical situation, the Filipino people are a heterogeneous group. We speak different languages, we live on different islands, we have different cultures. Our geographical location places us in Southeast Asia but our history brings us closer to Spanish and American ways of life as well as those of some of our Asian neighbors. It seems to me then that, because of our heritage, being Filipino is necessarily to be diverse. In fact, it is our diversity that gives us our identity as a people. For Christianity to be Filipino, therefore, it must necessarily be diverse. It must take serious account of our cultural differences and our different ways of expressing ourselves. Whether one is talking of liturgical celebrations or doctrinal expressions of faith, Christianity in the Philippines must seriously take account of "the differences which give us our identity." I believe this is why Filipino Christian theologians are wrestling with what has been called "inculturation" since it would be a pity if the way we portray our Christian beliefs is ignored simply because we have chosen to turn to our different cultures to articulate those beliefs. It would be unfortunate if we did not dare to let our cultural differences help us to understand the Christian message. Since there is a sense in which Christianity is culture-bound, Filipino cultures (our indigenous cultures: Tagalog, Ilocano, Visayan, Bicolano and so on) are just as acceptable in expressing Christianity. The challenge is how to show that point and, more importantly, how to take up that challenge.

Culture is about our experience as a people. Unfortunately, a large part of that experience for the majority of the Filipinos is poverty, oppression and exploitation. This is why Philippine Christianity, if it is to speak to our present life, must address this issue. An important aspect of that responsibility is identifying the causes of the sad plight of our people. An even more significant part is taking a stand. If Christianity is to be credible in the Philippines it must be seen as actively working to bring about a situation that will enable us to live a human kind of existence. Why? When he was asked this very question in connection with his role at the EDSA event, Cardinal Sin asked another question: "Have you ever seen a soul walking about?" In other words, we are dealing with human beings, not disembodied spirits. The needs of the Filipinos as human beings are our Christian concern. Because poverty and injustice hinder them from living human lives, Christianity's task in the Philippines also involves working to transform that situation.

Finally, in saying that Christianity in the Philippines should be a message of hope, I am aware of the difficulties that that challenge presents. How can we credibly assure our people that we must continue working because there is a brighter future? There is nothing worse than delivering empty promises. And as some philosophers have been reminding us, the Christian religion is particularly susceptible to this criticism. How can we re-kindle hope in those who have been de-humanized? How can we truly show that Christianity can make a difference to our lives? What realistic basis do we have in our Christian heritage to substantiate our claim for a better tomorrow? Perhaps it is easier to discuss inculturation or even to actively support the process of liberation than it is to justify people's expectations. In fact, some would cynically point out that EDSA failed to meet people's expectations. Will Christianity in the Philippines suffer the same fate? Yet providing a real basis for hope and working for its fulfillment is essential. It is a task that cannot be legitimately ignored just because, for whatever reasons, there have been failures in the past or because the Christian message has not always been forthright about it. In my opinion, this task is one of the biggest challenges in the Philippines today for those of us who profess to be Christians.

The Nature of a Legacy

I have described Philippine Christianity as a legacy from Spanish times. It is in the nature of any legacy that while its origins are in the past, it has survived into the present. In many cases a legacy is something to be treasured. But it is also possible for it to be nothing else but "a dead weight" and therefore to be discarded in one way or another. I am sure that there are those who believe that what has been handed down to us by the Spaniards, namely Christianity, is one such "dead weight" best put aside or even resisted. In fact, there are some who would maintain that it is what is impeding the country's development and therefore Filipinos should free themselves from its influence just as they had managed to release Spain's hold on us in 1898.

There is no doubt that there are a number of negative sides to this legacy—it is not necessary to mention them here. Still, I maintain that, unlike other legacies, Philippine Christianity—because it is a living force—is the same legacy that has enabled us to continue to make whatever contribution Filipinos in various areas have been able to offer in the last hundred years. We are what we are because of our history, and that history—for the majority of Filipinos—includes the Christianity left to us by Spain. In fact, I believe that we are able to see the shortcomings of that legacy precisely because the same legacy did teach us something; namely, that the Christian message is more than just what we have learned specifically from the Spanish version of it. The task is not to get rid of that legacy, but to let it significantly bring about a brighter future. That I hope can be one of the accomplishments of this centennial celebration.

NOTES

1. The Greeks had two different words for "time": *kronos* meaning the passage of time, and *kairos* meaning time as opportunity. It is in the sense of KAIROS that I understand a centennial celebration to be inasmuch as it is marking more than the mere passage of a hundred years.

2. As the collection of essays in Gerard H. Anderson (ed.), *Studies in Philippine Church History* (Ithaca and London: Cornell University Press, 1969) shows, Christianity in the Philippines during Spanish times can hardly be characterized as monolithic. There were differences among the religious orders and between them and the bishops. There were conflicts with civil power and with other groups.

3. John Leddy Phelan provides such a study in his *The Hispanization of the Philippines: Spanish Aims and Filipino Responses 1565-1700* (Madison: University of Wisconsin Press, 1959).

4. The EDSA event, with its power to motivate the ordinary people, bears some comparison with the *Pasyon* as interpreted by Reynaldo Clemena Ileto. See his, *Pasyon and Revolution: Popular Movements in the Philippines 1840-1910* (Quezon City: Ateneo de Manila University Press, 1979).

5. See, for example, Fr. John N. Schumacher's illuminating study, *Revolutionary Clergy: The Filipino Clergy and the Nationalist Movement 1850-1903* (Quezon City: R. P. Garcia Publishing Co., 1990).

6. For an assessment of the impact of the Marcos regime on the political, economic, and social life of the Filipinos and the implications for Americans, cf. John Bresnan (ed.), *Crisis in the Philippines: The Marcos Era and Beyond* (Princeton, NJ: Princeton University Press, 1986).

OF PHOTOGRAPHS
AND COUNTRY ROADS

John L. Silva

Since 1996 the Philippines has plodded through a series of significant one hundred year commemorations highlighting the country's revolt against the Spaniards and the establishment of a sovereign government. Many of the events involved dramatic battle reenactments, unveiling of historical markers, and the requisite parades. In more than a few instances, the events have been sparsely attended save only by paid government employees and students hauled in for the occasion. Despite full page advertisements appearing in newspapers heralding the day's importance, the lackluster and forced attendance gives the advertisements a "post-it notes" quality. Noted today. Forgotten tomorrow.

Former President Fidel Ramos, who once faced an empty grandstand audience during one of those events, lamented the low awareness levels among the citizenry over the centennial. Columnists and scholars have pointed their fingers at a variety of reasons for this national lethargy. The high point for this year's centennial, the proclaiming of the Philippine Republic on June 12, 1898, had grand floats each portraying the country's history, from muscled chieftains of pre-Spanish times to the clenched fists of the People Power Revolution of 1986. In the evening, a massive fireworks display sparkled and banged over Manila Bay. For this one day, a whole country celebrated its national birth, entranced more by pageantry and colors and less by thoughtful reflection.

After June 12th, the hyped and tenuously sustained attempt of continuing the centennial celebrations have faltered if not imploded. Since then, the commemorative newspaper advertisements are fewer; the centennial spirit further dispirited despite the country's centennial commission extending the commemorations another three years. Meanwhile the country limps and hobbles through the remainder of this year, with *barongs* and *piña* dresses facing a dwindling round of stiff celebrations and dry cleaners. And hanging obscenely on telephone poles and street lights are ragged and dirty Filipino flags, abandoned and forgotten. It seems too much of an exertion to take them down, reverently fold them or display them in a manner befitting a national symbol's 100th painful year.

‡ ‡ ‡

I drive to work to a museum full of photographs of the Philippines taken one hundred and more years ago. Throughout the day, I gaze at images of how people lived then, how the landscape looked like, what the quality of life was during that period. When I drive back to Manila at the end of a day, I can't help but contrast and compare what this country and its people have undergone in a hundred years.

To celebrate a centennial is not only to reenact events or rehash eulogies. Marking a centennial is to survey a country's progress, reviewing in the process the vision and aspirations of past heroes and heroines. Photographs of a country's past allow a people to reflect what has been achieved. Photographs as well reveal what a country has not realized which could explain the seeming nationwide stupor over the myriad of centennial events.

Country road in turn–of–the century Philippines

The ambiance in 19th century photographs of street scenes and pathways are significant for their languor and lack of haste. Vendors calmly pose in the middle of a tree-lined street with no horse drawn vehicles in sight. Shy *señoritas* clutching their *ternos*, suspended in time and motion, glide across an empty cobbled street, open fans held up to shade their faces. Even on the main business street called Escolta, *carromatas* and *calesas* amble on freely and unhampered.

Today, when I drive on General Aguinaldo Highway, in Cavite, I navigate on a very dense and, oftentimes, jammed roadway. I will invariably pass a mother and child, or an old woman clutching to a companion, standing at the center of the unlined, undivided highway, buses recklessly whizzing by in both directions just inches away from them. Thick black exhaust fumes envelope them and as they press handkerchiefs tightly to their faces, they glance at me and my oncoming vehicle with fear and resigned horror. These same people whose forefathers routed the Spanish in many battles are in the middle of a highway, named after their favored son, scared and wondering if they'll cross the highway alive. Instead of the gentle, sublime faces found in old photographs, the more familiar pose these days are of people resembling bank robbers as blackened face towels, ski masks, and even an occasional gas mask are strapped permanently to their faces.

Unhurried placid faces on the streets or in *carromatas*, of a hundred years ago, have been replaced with faces on the street looking quite forlorn, waiting interminably for a jeepney to get them to school, or to work, or to a ramshackled home.

When they manage to miraculously squeeze onto a seat, they are mercilessly jostled and bounced violently in decrepit vehicles driven by homicidal maniacs with a death wish. The legacy for the descendants of *Katipuneros* is to risk their lives each day to filthy air, murderous transports, and the demeaning emptiness of waiting.

Old photographs of the Pasig River show a languid, serene river snaking past grand country homes and fertile rice fields. Fishing rafts lower their nets into a pristine water while *cascos* and *lorchas* down river, closer to the mouth, unload goods and passengers. *Esteros* and waterways leading to the river recall Venetian settings as *bancas* glide under quaint arched bridges while onlookers cast a languorous gaze upon the drifting scenery. The cool breeze the river induces, the mirrored reflection on the water of moon and stars at night inspired much 19th century poetry and musical compositions. Jose Rizal, while traveling on a European river would recall and pine for his Pasig River.

The old Pasig River photographs hanging on our museum walls arouse audible sighs and exasperated exclamations as viewers decry the horrible sewage that has become the Pasig River today. There is a note of shock because it is now a fourth or fifth generation of Filipinos who've seen the river as putrid and inhospitable. A whole country has never known the river to be clean that upon reading past romantic odes and verses about the Pasig, they wonder if there has been some geographical error.

There is a picture of the last Spanish Governor General poised in his open carriage, with his livery and footmen ready to be pulled by four horses away from the portico of Malacañang Palace. He is, from the cast of an afternoon light, headed for Bagumbayan, now Luneta, where a daily ritual of a promenade at dusk is about to start on an oval gravel path fronting Manila Bay.

As custom would have it, all carriages and strollers on the Luneta traveled in one direction around the roadway. The Governor-General's carriage would traverse solely in the opposite direction in order that carriage passengers and passing strollers greet, bow, or salute this despised symbol of Spanish authority.

Escolta, Manila circa 1899

Driving on the highway, I will occasionally see ahead a flashing of lights barreling towards me on my imaginary lane. They are massive four wheel drives or very expensive cars with the darkest of tinted windshields. On their roofs are whirling colored lights and from their engine emanates a warbled siren piercing the air in shrilled fury. The vehicles, finding the traffic jam on their lane beneath them, have crossed over to my lane; and their sound and light gadgets give them, for a brief second, the pseudo-license of being the law or being an ambulance. But they are neither. They are just imperious and arrogant and their urgency a sham as they plow my vehicle and the vehicles behind me aside while luckless smoldering citizens view this yet another indignity and must swallow their departing dust and carbon. This forced obeisance reminds me of the Governor General and his carriage. Our forefathers were riled into revolution by the aloofness of the Iberian Governor and a hundred years later the aggravation continues, this time by so many more petty tyrants with equivalent skin tones. Everyone, even funeral car owners can pick up one of these twirling light devices at the neighborhood hardware store and become, in an instant, another despised homegrown *hijo de puta*.

Cameras then couldn't capture in detail the fineries Filipinos wore, especially those of fine pineapple fiber. Exquisite embroidery and marvelous patterns are oftentimes lost in fading albumen prints. But verities remain: the photographic eye captured a people, from women cigar rollers, to male servants, to idle *mestizas*, all swathed in elegant translucent *piña*, those shadowy, flimsy gauze hinting of erotic bodies within to the consternation of dour and lascivious friars.

A young Filipina dressed in traditional attire, circa 1899

Bulbous shouldered; chemise patterned with one sleeve hanging perilously over one shoulder; crinkled stiff *barongs* or pineapple fiber languorously draped over bosoms, the fashion statement then was a people who dressed for the divine pleasure of vanity and tropical convenience.

Today, Filipinos still retain a verve for dressing. Our fashion ramps, cocktail parties and glittering affairs are undiminished in panache and style. But the pizzazz is limited; unlike the past where even the poorest could wrap themselves in indigenous swirls of colors, today the marginal folk make do with hand-me-downs alien to their location. An old provincial man framed in swaying bamboo trees now sports a frayed t-shirt emblazoned with the jarring name of Tommy Hilfiger or Jurassic Park or University of Alabama. A whole country unmindful of the products emblazoned on their t-shirts. Where once there was proportion, sleekness, and complementary accessories to dressing, today anarchy exists as uniformed school girls sport baseball caps turned backwards, vulgar jewelry is worn by the *parvenu,* and ill fitting suits are *de rigueur.*

Many 19th century photographers, like painters, captured pastoral, rural scenes mindful of the creeping and ugly industrialization they witnessed in their European cities. When photographers traveled to distant lands including the Philippines, their eyes wandered, searching to compose a scene both exotic and as a visual paean to the last undisturbed shores of nature.

Some of the finest panoramas of idyllic countrysides were taken from the top of a hill or from a church tower. Beneath wide swaths of coconut and acacia trees, thatched roofs appear in the near distance while a blanket of vegetation and trees extend outward as far as the eye can see. The relationship between inhabitant and surroundings then was not symbiotic. Nature, not man, held sway, from the night canopy of brilliant stars above to the depths of the opal seas below.

The insignificant number of six million souls have, a century hence, quantified almost ten times; their presence on the speckled island republic have been felt more as a blight than as stewards of a fragile land. The stars no longer flicker their brilliance; they are hidden in the deadly combustion and detritus we spew to the air. Once an animistic people who conversed with trees for permission to pass or to break a branch, today, hardly a tree is left to offer a greeting. We are undeterred in a killing spree as we molest the once opal waters by dynamiting corals and pouring acid on them to stun, steal, and export the most colorful and therefore pitiful of fishes.

I survey the roomful of photographs before dimming the lights which signals our museum guards of the day's end. In the blur of one long sweep of the eyes, images come forth from their frames. The peaceful Pasig, the simple huts, the languorous smiles, these time-locked visuals remain with me as I board my car to drive home on styrofoam littered roads and plastic bags swirling about. The lights shining above are not the stars but searchlights from contruction cranes. I drive past people cupping their mouths and squinting their eyes from the gritty toxic air.

In this *fin de siecle* moment, one is hard pressed finding reasons to celebrate our national existence. Did our forefathers declare war and proclaim nationhood only for its descendants to savage its patrimony? For the next one hundred years, have we left a legacy of imbecilic children addled-brained with malnutrition, lead emission, and airplane glue?

It is the end of November and I take a Sunday drive away from the city, on roads impassable and forgotten. The cool wind from China clears the air and the views from atop a ridge are crisp and clear. I cross a small bridge and the creek below is flanked by arching bamboo trees and suffused with the gurgling water from the morning rains. I remember an old photograph of a similar scene. My jeep bounces about through a grove of mango trees past a man tugging at his carabao hitched to a sled carrying palm leaves. A boy, in his Sunday best appears mysteriously from the shadows of canefields bearing an armful of yellow haliconias. A gathering of elderly men and women with wrinkled faces and puckered smiles gather seated on benches outside a simple thatched store.

I reach the sea and from the shore I recognize a distant island still unspoiled, the very same one found in a 17th century map on our museum wall. I look at the shore lined with coconut trees, a common scene throughout the islands and described by Magellan's chronicler Pigafetta upon their first and ominous landing. There is no blanket of poisoned air here and the afternoon sun casts a red-orange glow on fishermen in their boats and the people on shore. Pigafetta would describe these natives as being peaceful, were of goodwill, and conscientious.

Away from the arteries leading to the metropole, away from the cacophony of urban sprawl, I am heartened to be in wide stretches of emerald green ricefields and verdant hills. It is soothing to see a blanket of green for my generation is just two decades removed from this familiar sight. My high school in a subdivision on the outskirts of Manila was once surrounded by rice fields and grazing carabaos. Now the area is part of Metro Manila and the fields concretized into three gigantic shopping malls. The lone highway to that school have sprouted tentacles of overpasses and underpasses. On an 1894 map of Manila, the evident signs of population are on the gridded streets of the walled city of Intramuros. Surrounding the fortress city is an expanse of green coloring with meandering lines signifying the boundaries of each rice field. Save for Intramuros and the adjoining promenade of Bagumbayan where malevolent carriages circled and heroes executed, the outlying districts were but stretches of glistening, sprouting rice stalks in glimmering wet fields.

If Manila and the other cities have been the venues of centennial celebrations, exhibitions, and fireworks, it is the countryside that recalls an earlier topography and social setting. It is there, miraculously unspoiled and languid where one ruminates the passing of time and the challenges faced by a resilient people for the next millennium. In old photographs and distant provincial roads—away from the din, ephemeral gunpowder and political exhortations—there lie the unlocked stories of our one hundred years.

1 0 0 Years
of Philippine
Education

{ I I }

THE MARRIAGE OF MARIA CLARA AND UNCLE SAM: COLONIALISM AND THE EDUCATION OF FILIPINOS

Edmundo F. Litton

Throughout history, Filipinos have been influenced by foreigners. The strategic location of the Philippines made the country easy conquest for colonizers (Zaide 1966). Thus, when one analyzes the educational experiences of Filipinos in the Philippines and in the United States, it is clear that one needs to consider the colonial past of the Filipinos. Colonialism has had an impact on issues relating to identity, language, and education. The image of a marriage between fictional characters, Maria Clara and Uncle Sam, is a fitting metaphor of the educational experience of Filipinos in the Philippines and in the United States. Maria Clara is the main character in Jose Rizal's historical novel, *Noli Me Tangere*. Maria Clara is the personification of the Philippines. Rizal described Maria Clara as the picture of innocence. Uncle Sam, on the other hand represents the United States. This paper will explore the results of this marriage between colonizer and colonized and the impact this relationship has had on the education of Filipinos.

Molding Maria Clara: Foreign Influence on Filipino culture

Colonization has had a tremendous effect on the Philippines. Many Filipinos can share Memmi's (1965) sentiments when he says "I discovered that few aspects of my life and personality were untouched by [colonization]. Not only my own thoughts, my passions, and my conduct, but also the conduct of others towards me was affected." (viii). Though the era of colonization ended in the Philippines almost half a century ago, its effects continue to be felt even today.

The Spaniards stayed in the Philippines for over three centuries and the Americans exerted their influence for half a century. The Spaniards colonized the Philippines in the name of "three G's—God, Gold, and Glory" (Zaide 1966). Spanish colonization in the Philippines ended with the Spaniards' loss to the Americans in the Spanish-American war of 1898. This defeat was the start of the American colonization of the Philippines, "or as the neat summation of Philippines history goes: three centuries in a Catholic convent and fifty years in Hollywood." (Karnow 1989:9)

Different from the European colonizers, the Americans "were uniquely benign, almost sentimental imperialists" (Karnow 1989:13). The United States government granted independence to the Philippines shortly after the defeat of the Japanese by the American forces in the Pacific. On July 4, 1946, "for the first time in history, an imperial nation was voluntarily relinquishing a possession as the United States kept its pledge to emancipate the Philippines." (Karnow 1989:323). Karnow (1989) further states that this peaceful transition was unlike other colonial transitions in Asia. The Indonesians defied the Dutch, the Vietnamese prepared to reassert their power over the French, and resistance against the British intensified in India and in Malaysia. The amicable departure of the Americans is one of the reasons why many Filipinos continued to treat the United States as a "friend" after the era of colonization.

Even before the Spaniards and Americans colonized the Philippines, the Filipinos shared the culture of many of their Malay neighbors. Ponce (1980) states that the Malay, Spanish, and American experiences are three major factors that have shaped Philippine society and culture. The Malay influence is seen in the Filipino's belief in magic, animism, fatalism, and the belief in the extended family. The Spanish influence is evident in the Filipino's practice of Catholicism, class consciousness, and a profound respect for authority figures. The American influence is evident in the Filipino's desire for democratic ideals, the use of English as a major language, and the adoption of American styles of dress, music, and arts. At first glance, these multiple influences can be seen as contradictory. When the American influence is strongest, Filipinos display a love for democracy, Filipinos delight in being able to speak English, or Filipinos may boast at wearing the latest in American fashions. However, at other times, the Spanish influence may be more evident in the form of religious practices and attitudes, acceptance of class differences, and a belief in the superiority of anything foreign. When the Malay influence is heaviest, Filipinos may become superstitious, animistic, and fatalistic. As a result of these conflicting influences, which can often operate simultaneously, "the Filipino can be seen—even by other Filipinos—as inconsistent and contradictory (Ponce 1980:160).

Educating Maria Clara: Education of Filipinos During the Colonial Period

An educational system is one of the first things that both the Spaniards and Americans created when they arrived in the Philippines. Schools served a variety of purposes for the Spaniards and Americans. Schools were not used solely to educate the Filipinos. Education was also used as a tool to create divisions in society between the rich and the poor.

The Spaniards introduced a western system of education (Cortes 1980; Carson 1978). Under Spanish rule, the Philippines saw the birth of numerous universities and colleges in Manila. The University of Santo Tomas was founded by the Dominican friars in 1601. The Society of Jesus established the Ateneo de Manila University. The institutions established during the Spanish colonial period were tools for sharing European art, literature and music in the Philippines. The Spanish friars also operated other public schools that had Catholic doctrine as the main emphasis in the curricula.

The educational contributions by Spain, however, should be seen in the light of the effects of colonialism. While the Spaniards established a formal educational system, Karnow (1989) notes that most of these institutions admitted only young Spaniards who were training for the priesthood. The rural schools for the native Filipinos were usually inadequate schools run by priests. The priests "taught the catechism and the lives of the saints, submitting their pupils to inane interrogations, recited in unison and heavily dosed with discipline." (Karnow 1989:52). These classes were all conducted in the local languages of the people "on the principle that fluency in Spanish would make the indios uppity and arrogant." (Karnow 1989:53) Thus, while the Spaniards introduced some helpful changes to Filipino society, the real reasons for this assistance should not be forgotten.

Memmi (1965) notes that "if [the colonizer] wants to help the colonized, it is exactly because their destiny concerns him . . . because he hopes to go on living in the colony." (36) The educational contributions of Spain lead to believe that the Spanish occupation modernized the "primitive" Filipino. Rimonte (1997) captures the commonly held view of Spanish colonialism:

As a result, Filipinos have never doubted the dominant view that Europeans risked their lives to voyage thousands of miles from Mexico—over largely uncharted seas, in death-defying ships, enduring the hardships of legend and nightmare at enormous costs to the Spanish king's personal treasury—just to bring the gift of their religion. For our own good, the colonizers did what nobility obliged them to do (40).

The American government brought education to all people in the Philippines. Education, under the American occupation, was no longer solely for the elite. Consistent with American colonial policy, education was used as a tool for molding Filipinos to adhere to the image of an ideal American (Strobel 1996). The educational system was not established by the Americans for the sole purpose of enlightening the Filipinos. Consistent with the purposes of American colonial policy, the goal of education was to train the Filipinos to be citizens of an American colony (Makol-Abdul 1997). The first American teachers were soldiers. Later on the "Thomasites" arrived. These teachers were named after the ship they used to sail to the Philippines, the *SS Thomas.*

Unlike the Spaniards, who delivered education in the languages of the people, English was the medium of instruction in the American educational system (Galang 1988). Llamzon (1970) cites that none of the existing languages could be used because there were no educational materials available in the local languages. Furthermore, a neutral language, English, had to be introduced to squelch the regional jealousy that existed. Marasigan (1986) notes that "the choice of English was considered reasonable and was whole-heartedly accepted by the people (338). Thus, all educational materials were imported from the United States. Images of America as the "land of milk and honey" were portrayed in the textbooks that were used. Filipinos were taught to emulate the American lifestyle and to live the American dream. Everything "American" was supposed to be good. After all, the United States "saved" the Filipinos from centuries of Spanish rule and the Americans liberated the Philippines from the Japanese occupation during World War II.

The introduction of English was the first step in an attempt to "Americanize" the Filipinos. William McKinley once told a group of clergymen that "God told him to annex the [Philippine] islands." (Karnow 1989:11). Like most colonists, the Americans saw the Filipinos as inferior. Karnow (1989) notes that William Howad Taft "went to Manila with the preconceived notion that the Filipinos were unsuited to govern themselves" (19). However, assimilation was never achieved. While Memmi (1965) notes that assimilation is an alternative for the colonized as long as he tolerates colonization, assimilation is always refused by the colonizers. This sentiment is best reflected in a song composed by an American soldier:

They say I've got brown brothers here,
But I still draw the line
He may be a brother of Big Bill Taft
But he ain't no brother of mine
(Karnow 1989:174)

The American government, unlike the Spanish government, promised that one day the Philippines would be independent. This proclamation, however, was not for the benefit of the Filipinos. Miller (1982) narrates that the occupation of the Philippines was met with mixed feelings in the United States. While some cheered at the growth of American imperialism, others saw it as a moral evil. Independence eventually came to the people of the Philippine islands in 1946, shortly after the end of World War II.

The American educational policy, however, was detrimental to the indigenous people of Mindanao. Most of the people living in Mindanao are Muslim. The colonial system of education failed to attract a majority of the Muslims because the system was imbued with Christian values (Makol-Abdul 1997). Accepting American education was seen as cultural suicide for the Muslims. The American educational system was associated with teaching values that were contradictory to Islamic ideals. Thus, the Muslims did not learn how to survive in the new system. They started to lag behind their Christian counterparts and were often prone to exploitation and oppression.

The development of the educational system during the colonial era in the Philippines should be seen in light of the purposes of colonialism. Both the Spaniards and Americans can be credited for influencing the systematic delivery of education to Filipinos.

Maria Clara After the Conquest: The Effects of Colonialism on Filipino Life

The effects of the Spanish and American colonization can still be felt in the Philippines. Many Filipinos have Spanish surnames (such as Benedicto, Del Castillo, Del Rosario, Santos, or Santiago). Many Filipinos have European physical features including light skin and a sharp nose. But because of the negative image of Spain, many

Filipinos quickly abandoned their Spanish heritage including speaking Spanish.

The effects of American colonialism are still evident in the Philippines. Despite the closure of the American bases in the mid 1990s, the influence of the United States is still evident in everyday life of Filipinos especially in the capital city of Manila. Many buildings in the capital were influenced by American architects. Many of the suburbs have affluent neighborhoods that resemble Beverly Hills. Popular American fast-food chains have established restaurants in major cities of the Philippines. Karnow (1989) cites Philippine author, Carmen Guerrero Nakpil, who observes that many Filipino families try to emulate the American lifestyle by furnishing their homes with leather furniture, wool rugs, and fur pillows. All of these items are not practical in the Philippines because of the high humidity year round. During the Christmas holidays, some Filipinos spray their windows with fake snow. Nakpil reports that as a child she wondered how Santa Claus could deliver presents on Christmas as Filipino homes did not have chimneys. In the Philippines, there is also much prestige attached to the "Made in the USA" label. While many American products are made under license in the Philippines, many Filipinos drive long distances to the site of the former American bases to purchase the same products made in the United States (Karnow 1989).

The years of colonialism has indoctrinated Filipinos with the image of America as the land of milk and honey. Filipinos comprise one of the largest and fastest growing immigrant groups in the United States (Strobel 1996; Fermin 1991), with Philippine immigration being second only to that of Mexico. *Balikbayans* or returning Filipinos from the United States are often given a hero's welcome on their return to the Philippines. Filipinos in the United States are often thought of us those who "have made it." Life in the United States, however, is not all that it is made up to be and many Filipinos often suffer discrimination and underemployment in America.

Colonialism is most evident in the language situation of Filipinos in the United States and in the Philippines. English is spoken by many Filipinos. Proficiency in English is often associated with higher social status. Many American television shows are broadcast in the Philippines. Road signs are in English. Many classes, even in rural areas, are taught in English. Despite the desire to become more nationalistic, many Filipinos are reluctant to give up learning English because English proficiency is seen as a tool for economic mobility. The ability to speak English allows Filipinos to work abroad (Sevilla 1988) and interact with foreigners. Memmi (1965) explains that "possession of two languages is not merely a matter of having two tools, but actually means participation in two physical and cultural realms" (107). In the United States, the biggest obstacle to maintaining Philippine languages in the Filipino community comes from the Filipinos themselves. Many immigrant families immediately begin to use English as the language of the home. In her study of attitudes towards bilingual education in the Filipino-American community, Juarez (1997) notes that the opposition to using Filipino as a language of instruction is a product of the Filipino's colonial mentality. While Filipinos see the importance of being able to speak more than one language, the participants in the study preferred that their children learn English and Spanish—not Filipino.

Colonialism has had a tremendous effect on Filipino culture. Colonialism taught Filipinos to see their culture as second rate to the cultures of the colonizers. This has led to an identity crisis. Revilla (1997) notes, "For many young Filipinos today, the identity crisis revolves around the lack of self-respect and self-love as Filipinos"

(101). Revilla (1997) further states, the identity is also affected by physical appearance. Years of colonialism, has led to intermarriages. What is a Filipino supposed to look like? Filipinos of mixed heritage may feel that they do not belong to any of the ethnic groups that make up the Filipino heritage.

Future Directions: Celebrating the Past

Filipinos have been through a tremendous journey over the last 100 years and the next 100 years promises to be just as exciting as the last century. Foreigners have invaded the Philippines and left their mark on Filipino culture and have contributed to the education of Filipinos. While there have been periods of bliss in the marriage between colonizer and colonized, there have also been times of great turmoil. Filipinos need to acknowledge the past and move on. The important task of the Filipino people is "to rebuild his people, what-ever be their authentic nature; to reform their unity, communicate with it and to feel that they belong" (Memmi 1965:135). Filipinos need to rediscover their rich cultural heritage and develop a more pos-itive attitude towards Philippine languages. Philippine languages should be seen as a tool for celebrating the Filipino life and culture.

Filipinos have so much of which to be proud. Filipinos can look at the past and acknowledge the accomplishments of those who have contributed to what the Philippines is today. A song-poem of the Shaman (as cited in Carew 1988) best exemplifies the need to be grateful for all those who have made the Philippines free in spirit:

Tread softly for numberless
dark ancestors sleep under the earth
and if perchance you press your ear

to the ground on moon-bright nights
echoes of long time past sorrows
will swirl inside your head
splashes of sunlight and shadows
will partner trade winds
Listen well,
You'll hear a rollcall of
heroes, heroines, and hosts
of the innocent dead
Make your footfalls
Lighter than a jaguar's
for every spot on earth
You touch is an
Unmarked ancestral grave
(p. 115)

REFERENCES

Carew, John. 1966. *Fulcrums of Change: Origins of Racism in the Americas and Other Essays.* Trenton, NJ: Africa World Press, Inc.

Carson, Arthur L. 1978. *The Story of Philippine Education.* Quezon City, Philippines: New Day Publishers.

Cortes, J. R. 1980. The Philippines. In T. N. Postlewaite & R. M. Thomas, eds. *Schooling in the ASEAN Region: Indonesia, Malaysia, the Philippines, Singapore, Thailand.* New York: Pergamon Press.

Galang, Rosita. 1988. The Language Situation of Filipino Americans. In Sandra Lee McKay and Sau-ling Cynthia Wong, eds. *Language diversity, problem or resource.* Cambridge: Newbury House Publishers.

Jaurez, Leni. 1997. *Attitudes of Filipino Parents in the United States towards Bilingual Education.* Unpublished doctoral dissertation, University of San Francisco.

Karnow, Stanley. 1989. *In Our Image: America's Empire in the Philippines.* New York: Random House.

Llamzon, Teodoro. 1970. On the Medium of Instruction: English or Pilipino. *Philippine Studies* 18(3), 683-694

Makol-Abdul, Pute Rahimah. 1997 Colonialism and Change: The Case of Muslims in the Philippines. *Journal of Muslim Minority Affairs* 17(2), 311-324.

Marasigan, Elizabeth. 1986. A note on Philippine mix-mix. *Philippine Studies* 34(3), 338-359.

Memmi, Albert. 1965. *The Colonizer and the Colonized.* New York: Orion Press.

Miller, Stuart Creighton. 1982. *Benevolent Assimilation.* New Haven and London: Yale University Press.

Ponce, D. E. 1980. Introduction: The Philippine background. In J. F. McDermott, Jr., W. Tseng, & T. W. Maretzki, eds. *People and Cultures of Hawaii: A psycho-cultural profile.* Honolulu: Jon A. Burns School of Medicine and the University of Hawaii Press.

Revilla, Linda A. 1997 Filipino American Identity: Transcending The Crisis. In Maria P. P. Root, ed. *Filipino Americans: Transformation and Identity.* Thousand Oaks, London, and New Delhi: Sage Publications.

Rimonte, Nilda. 1997. Colonialism's Legacy: The Inferiorizing of the Filipino. In Maria P. P. Root, ed. *Filipino Americans: Transformation and Identity.* Thousand Oaks, London, and New Delhi: Sage Publications.

Sevilla, J. C. 1988. Level of Awareness of the Bilingual Education Policy among Parents and among Government and non-Government Organizations. In Bonifacio P. Sibayan and Andrew Gonzalez, eds. *Evaluating Bilingual Education in the Philippines* (1974-1985). Manila, Philippines: Linguistic Society of the Philippines.

Strobel, Elenita. 1996. *Coming Full Circle: The Process of Decolonization Among Post-1965 Filipino Americans.* Unpublished doctoral dissertation, University of San Francisco.

Zaide, Gregorio F. 1966. *Republic of the Philippines.* Manila: Rex Book Store.

LANGUAGE OF INSTRUCTION IN THE PHILIPPINES IN THE TWENTIETH CENTURY: POLICIES, ORIENTATIONS, AND FUTURE DIRECTIONS

Rosita G. Galang

Introduction

The nature of language planning efforts in any particular setting is influenced by the basic orientations toward language and its role and toward languages and their role in society (Ruiz 1988). Language may be referred to as "a means or a tool" (Tauli 1974), as "sentimental attachment" (Kelman 1972), or as "problem, right, or resource" (Ruiz 1988). In this paper the language of instruction policies in the Philippines from 1898 to 1998 are presented within the context of the language situation in the country and then discussed in terms of their orientations and future directions.

Language Situation in the Philippines

The language situation in the Philippines is a complex one. This complexity may be attributed to linguistic, sociological, political, and educational factors including, but not limited to, the number and diversity of languages spoken, the national language question, and the dilemma on the role and maintenance of English.

Linguistic Diversity. The Philippines consists of a "highly fragmented complex" of approximately 7,200 islands and islets off the southeast coast of mainland China. Rugged mountain ranges and an array of rivers on the larger islands tend to isolate the population, resulting in linguistic diversity. Estimates of the number of Philippine languages range from 100-150 (Llamzon 1978). Based on a possible subgrouping of Philippine languages, McFarland (1996) counted them in the sense of mutually unintelligible codes, and obtained a total of 110.

Although authorities differ on their count of Austronesian languages spoken in the Philippines, they agree on the eight indigenous languages designated as major regional languages because they are spoken natively by the eight largest ethnic groups. According to the 1970 Census of the Philippines, more than ninety percent of the population were speakers of these major languages which may be broken further into several dialects. English, which has served as an instructional medium for almost a century, is also widely spoken. Census data in 1972 indicated that about 34,000 influential people spoke English as a first language (Llamzon 1978). A language variety called "Standard Filipino English" has arisen from this situation (Llamzon 1972). There are also substantial numbers of speakers of Chinese and Arabic (Kaplan 1982). Table 1 shows the number of native speakers of the eight major languages (National Statistics Office 1990).

Table 1

Native Speakers of the Eight Major Languages of the Philippines

Language	No. of Speakers	Percentage of Population
1. Tagalog	16,910,458	27.9
2. Cebuano	14,709,844	24.3
3. Ilocano	5,923,514	9.8
4. Hiligaynon	5,647,067	9.3
5. Bicol	3,518,161	5.8
6. Waray	2,433,180	4.0
7. Pampango	1,897,319	3.1
8. Pangasinan	1,164,267	1.9

Five of the major languages (Tagalog, Ilocano, Bicol, Pampango, and Pangasinan) are spoken mainly in Luzon, the northern island; the remaining three are spoken in the Visayas, the central islands; and on the northern part of Mindanao, the southern island of the Philippines.

The National Language Question. The need for an indigenous national language, which was not proclaimed until 1937, is closely tied to the search for a national identity that commenced during the Spanish rule in the nineteenth century and continued during the American regime in the twentieth century. Social conflicts arising from the tension of competing languages are evidenced in the controversies over the national language question.

The Spanish colonizers (1565-1898) decreed that Spanish should be taught to the Filipino people. However, the Spanish missionaries found it easier to learn and use the indigenous languages of the population for evangelistic purposes. Thus, the friars who encouraged the Filipinos to give up their religion and adopt the Christian faith allowed them to retain their languages and encouraged but did not compel them to learn Spanish. The policy of encouragement was changed to that of obligation after 1688, but the policy was met with obstacles and was not successfully implemented (Phelan 1955). Access to Spanish was limited to native elites so that in the 1870 Census only 2.4 percent of the 4.7 million Filipinos spoke Spanish, although it remained an official language even through the American period, up to 1935 (Gonzalez 1980).

When the United States took over the Philippines from Spain (1898-1946), English was made the common language of communication and was added to Spanish as an official language (Beebe & Beebe 1981; Sibayan & Gonzalez 1990). English gradually replaced Spanish in influence so that according to the 1939 Census, more than 26.6 percent of the 16 million Filipinos spoke English (Gonzalez 1980).

Realizing the importance of language in the fight against the United States, the Japanese forces of occupation (1941-1945) took steps to downgrade the teaching of English and encouraged the use of Tagalog in schools and in government. They also organized Nippongo classes for government officials to further replace English (Sibayan & Gonzalez 1990).

The name of the national language has evolved from *Tagalog* or *Tagalog*-based to *Pilipino* to *Filipino*. *Tagalog* was proclaimed as the basis of the national language by President Manuel Quezon in 1937 with effectivity on December 30, 1939 following a mandate from the

1935 Constitution. The following year *Tagalog* was declared by the Commonwealth Act to be one of the official languages effective July 4,1946. Although only second to Cebuano in the number of speakers, *Tagalog* was spoken in Manila, the capital, and its surrounding areas. It was also considered as the most highly developed and studied indigenous language.

The *Tagalog*-based national language was renamed *Pilipino* by Secretary of Education Jose Romero in 1959 in order to free the national language of its ties with a particular ethnic group and to provide the language with the properties of a national symbol (Llamzon 1978). This was considered a necessary step since the regional connotations of the term *Tagalog* and the puristic tendencies of the propagators of the national language were seen as delaying its acceptance by the speakers of the other indigenous languages. Regionalism manifested in the opposition to *Pilipino* as the national language resurfaced during the preparatory hearings in 1971 and 1972 (Gonzalez 1996a). Ultimately, the 1973 constitution provided that "The National Assembly shall take steps toward the development and formal adoption of a common national language to be known as *Filipino*. Until otherwise provided by law, English and *Pilipino* shall be the official languages" (Juco 1977:10). The Philippine Constitution of 1987 declared *Filipino* to be the national language and provided that "As it evolves, it shall be further developed and enriched on the basis of existing Philippine and other languages" (Nolledo 1992:53).

The terms *Tagalog*, *Pilipino*, and *Filipino*, which have been used to refer to the national language of the Philippines, sometimes create confusion among those unfamiliar with the history of the Filipino language (Galang 1988). *Tagalog* is the indigenous Austronesian language on which the national language is based. The *Tagalog*-based national language was officially termed *Pilipino* in 1959. *Pilipino* is basically *Tagalog* enriched with officially recognized borrowed words primarily from English, Spanish, and Chinese; coinages; and revived words which have had differential success in popular usage. Many Filipinos did not perceive differences between *Tagalog* and *Pilipino* (Sibayan 1975), but in fact language planners have exerted conscious efforts to modify the regional language, e.g. by borrowing, to fulfill all the functions of a modern, national language, such as the transfer of scientific and technological information (Beebe & Beebe 1981; Gonzalez 1980; Laygo 1977). Increased use of *Pilipino* in the schools and mass media has led to the development of regional varieties of the national language which can no longer be identified exclusively as the language spoken in the Greater Manila area. *Pilipino* is expected to be spoken as a first or second language by at least 97.1 percent of the population by the year 2000 (Gonzalez 1996b).

Filipino, the approved national language of the Philippines since the ratification of the 1987 Constitution is *Tagalog*-based Pilipino enriched with lexical items from the indigenous and other languages spoken in the Philippines (Gonzalez 1988, 1996a; Nolledo 1992).

Dilemma on the Role and Maintenance of English. The current language situation in the Philippines presents a dilemma for Filipinos. On the one hand, the imperatives of nationalism demand that *Filipino*, the national language, be developed not only as a national *lingua franca*[1] but also as a language of education and scholarly discourse. On the other hand, economic, educational, and political considerations dictate the desirability of maintaining English (Gonzalez 1988).

The trend of the dissemination of *Filipino* indicates quite clearly its rapid expansion as a national *lingua franca* across the country and its expanding domain of use in the areas of Philippine life. At the same time, economic considerations suggest the maintenance of English for a substantial number of Filipinos. The Philippine Overseas Employment Administration continues to send workers abroad because of population growth and unemployment or under-employment in the country. Skills in the English language are need-ed not only for Filipinos' employability abroad, but also for the Philippines to maintain business and international relations, attract local investments, and encourage the transfer of regional offices in other Southeast Asian countries to Manila rather than Hong Kong or Singapore. Furthermore, access to science and technology for Filipinos is currently possible only through English which makes knowledge from the West available at an advanced level. The testi-mony of high school teachers, results of national tests, and observa-tions of classrooms have shown that there is now a generation of Filipinos conversant in *Filipino* but unable or unwilling to communi-cate in English, even after six years of instruction in English and *Filipino* (Gonzalez 1988).

Surveys have indicated that among Filipino parents, teachers, gov-ernment and non-government workers, and school administrators, the language of schooling or the mastery and use of the national language are not equated with nationalism. A bilingual instructional scheme in English and *Filipino* continues to be the majority choice and the choice of the *Tagalog*-based *Pilipino/Filipino* is no longer a divisive issue (Gonzalez 1988).

Similarly, Guerrero (1998) speaks of "a strange contradiction" in the interest expressed in the country regarding language teaching focused on the instructional medium in the schools. According to her, there seems to be a race among educational institutions to prepare/train English-speaking workers and professionals to meet the job requirements abroad, yet there is also a strong advocacy to develop the national language which will serve as the teaching medium so that the country will attain national progress and unity.

Past and Present Language of Instruction Policies

The history of the national language provides the background to the language policies in education in the Philippines. The country has experienced changes in the language of instruction initially dictated by colonizers to promote Christian faith and teach democratic ideals, and subsequently determined by Filipino policy makers in their efforts to promote quality education and unify the people through the use of a national language. The language of instruction policies which are discussed briefly in this section represent a century of changes starting with the policy of monolingual education in English (1898-1938) and ending with the current policy of full bilingual education (1974-1998). Gonzalez (1980) and Bernabe (1987) present a more comprehensive and detailed discussion of the Philippine experience in the area of language policy in education. Sibayan (1996a) describes in greater depth the stages of bilingual education in the Philippines.

Monolingual Instruction in English. From 1898 to 1938, English was used as the sole medium of instruction for all Filipinos in all subjects on all levels in all schools. English was introduced as the language of instruction in the Philippines by American soldiers in seven elementary schools in Manila on September 1, 1898. The Americans officially established the public school system in 1901 and the first boatload of school teachers called the "Thomasites" arrived and started mass education in English in 1902 (Llamzon 1978; Sibayan & Gonzalez 1990). While the 1935 Constitution of the Philippines provided that the law-making body of the country should take steps toward the development of a common national language based on one of the Philippine languages, the Tydings McDuffy Act mandated that during the Commonwealth period (1935-1945) an adequate system of public schools be established, maintained, and conducted primarily in English (Sibayan & Gonzalez 1990).

Bilingual Instruction in the Vernacular and English. On December 5, 1939, Secretary of Public Instruction Jorge Bocobo ordered that the native languages, which were barred from the schools, would be used as auxiliary media of instruction in Grades I and II when the child could not understand what was being taught in English. This was the first policy enunciated by a Filipino. In response to the 1935 Constitutional provision, the national language based on *Tagalog* was taught in the senior year of teacher education courses and in the fourth year high school beginning in 1940 (Sibayan & Gonzalez 1990).

In their efforts to replace English, the Japanese Imperial Forces (1941-1945) downgraded the teaching of English, encouraged the use of the *Tagalog*-based national language in schools and in government, and organized classes in Nippongo for government officials (Sibayan & Gonzalez 1990).

The use of the native languages as auxiliary media and the teaching of the *Tagalog*-based national language may be considered as the beginning of bilingual education in the Philippines. Experiments on the use of the vernacular[2] were conducted in the primary level of community schools, most notably in Iloilo and Bataan (Davis 1967; Prator 1950).

The success of these experiments led the Board of National Education to require the use of the vernacular as the medium of instruction and the introduction of English and *Pilipino* as subjects in Grades I and II, and the use of English as the language of instruction and *Pilipino* as an auxiliary medium from the third grade up to high school. This vernacular policy (1957-1973), which showed the official recognition of bilingualism in *Pilipino* and English in Philippine life, was rigidly implemented only in public schools. Many "elite" private schools were able to continue using English as the teaching medium from the first grade (Otanes 1974).

Bilingual Instruction in Pilipino/Filipino and English. In response to the desire and need of the people, especially student activists, to be competent in English and *Pilipino* in the late sixties and early seventies, the Board of National Education declared a policy on "bilingualism in the schools" in 1973. A year later, the guidelines for the implementation of the bilingual education policy were promulgated by the Department of Education and Culture (1974) with the purpose of developing a bilingual nation competent in *Pilipino* and English. Bilingual education was defined as "the separate use of *Pilipino* and English as media of instruction in definite subject areas, provided that additionally Arabic shall be used where it is necessary." According to this policy, *Pilipino* was to be used as the medium of instruction in social studies/social science, character education, work education, health education, and physical education. English was to be used to teach science, math, and English Communication Arts. The vernacular shall be the auxiliary medium in grades 1 and 2 only when necessary. English and *Pilipino* shall be taught as language subjects in all grades in the elementary and secondary schools. While schedules of implementation for *Tagalog* and non-*Tagalog* areas were different, there was none for tertiary institutions.

The Bilingual Education Policy enacted by the Department of Education, Culture and Sports (1987a, 1987b) essentially had the same provisions as the 1974 policy except for the following: the use of the regional languages as auxiliary media of instruction and as initial languages for literacy where needed; the task of tertiary level institutions to lead in the continuing intellectualization of Filipino; funds for policy implementation; and a more flexible timeline.

After eleven years of implementation (1974-1985) the Linguistic Society of the Philippines conducted a nationwide evaluation of bilingual education by assessing a sample of elementary school fourth and sixth graders and fourth year high school students across the archipelago in *Pilipino* and English as language subjects and in math, science, and social studies as content subjects. The evaluation team discovered a cross-sectional "deterioration" in achievement of pupils at the national level. Further examination of the data revealed that this dramatic deterioration in achievement was due not so much to bilingual schooling but to factors such as lack of teacher competence, type of community, socio-economic status, and institutional factors. The findings indicated a systemic problem beyond allocation for language and content subjects in *Pilipino* and English (Gonzalez & Sibayan 1988; Sibayan & Gonzalez 1990).

In 1991 the Congressional Commission on Education recommended the following:

1. Use of the vernacular as medium of instruction for all subjects in Grades 1-3, with *Filipino* as an auxiliary language of instruction, and a separate subject until fourth year high school; introduction of English as a separate subject in Grade 3 continuing until fourth year high school; use of *Filipino* as medium of instruction for all subjects, except English, in grade 4 until fourth year high school.

2. Language of instruction in tertiary education to be determined by individual institutions.

3. Switch to *Filipino* in technical-vocational education in the long term.

4. Development of a program by the Department of Education, Culture, and Sports for the preparation of instructional materials in *Filipino* so that by the year 2000, all subjects, except English and other languages, shall be taught in Filipino.

Basic Orientations Toward Languages and Their Role in Society

An examination of the language of instruction policies in the Philippines in the twentieth century reveals that different orientations toward languages and their role in Philippine society have had a significant impact upon policy formulation in the country.

Language policy makers' concern with the usefulness and efficiency of the vernaculars, the national language, and English as instructional media is indicative of an orientation toward language as a tool. The use of the "fairly undeveloped and unintellectualized" national language (Sibayan 1996b) as a medium of instruction may have been influenced by an orientation toward language as sentimental attachment. *Filipino*, the national language, has been chosen as a linguistic symbol of Filipino identity and unity though not without opposition from the non-*Tagalog* language groups.

From the past and present policies, it can be gleaned that problem-solving has dominated the educational language planning activity in the Philippines. It appears that within the context of national development, much of the work of language planners has been focused on the identification and resolution of language problems. In an update of the developments in language and nationalism in the Philippines, Gonzalez (1996a) pointed out that one of the insights from the Philippine experience of the past fifteen years (1973-88) is that "In a multi-ethnic society such as the Philippines, the selection of a vernacular on which to base the national language is fraught with problems that only time can solve" (233).

Bautista (1996) claims that the "language problem of the Philippines" is "reconciling the competing demands of ethnicity (= the vernacular), nationalism (= the national language), and modernization (= an international language)" (223). These observations are in consonance with Mackey's (1979) claim that "the more languages there are to choose from, the more complex the problems tend to become" (48) suggesting that language problems are inherent in a multilingual society.

The policy of monolingual instruction in English even at the expense of *Tagalog* and the other indigenous languages might have been based on the assumption that it was the solution to the problem of choosing the medium for teaching the ideals of democracy and making education accessible to a population speaking different languages. Similarly, the abandonment of the vernacular as the medium of instruction in the first two grades in 1974 might have been perceived as the solution to the problem of lack of trained teachers and instructional materials in the regional languages. The need for language training and materials production in the vernaculars coincided with the growing support for the search for a national symbol.

The mandate to use *Pilipino/Filipino* and English as media of instruction is a response to the population's desire and need to develop a bilingually competent nation where citizens speak the national language, the symbol of Filipino identity, and English, the link to the outside world, especially in the fields of science, technology, and business.

Partly due to the geographical features and the colonial history of the Philippines, the country is home to many whose mother tongue is not *Tagalog*, *Pilipino*, or *Filipino*, but one of the several Austronesian and other languages spoken in the country. More than half of the population speak natively languages other than *Tagalog*. Yet, little if at all, is being done to preserve these rich linguistic resources and use the experts to teach languages other than *Pilipino/Filipino* and English. It is also unfortunate that practically no steps are being taken to develop the population's language skills in the vernaculars. In fact, the government is doing little if at all, to promote the study of indigenous languages or encourage their maintenance. The result of this neglect of native languages in the Philippines could well be a pattern of language loss over just a few generations. The Philippines is a multilingual country, where speakers of many indigenous languages are expected to lose their first language.

Future Directions of Educational Language Planning

Considering the Philippine experience in educational language planning in the past hundred years, the country could benefit from an addition to her repertoire of orientations toward languages and their role in the Filipino society. Language-as-resource orientation is desirable in a multilingual context like the Philippines. This could provide a potentially important redirection for educational language planning, i.e. the integration of bilingual education into a responsible language policy for the country. Proceeding from language-as-resource orientation, language planners need to examine the role of the different languages in the context of the twenty-first century and take this into account when reviewing the current bilingual education policy. Instead of being a language shift policy for the speakers of languages other than *Filipino* and English, the policy could be modified so that it becomes a language maintenance and enrichment policy for all Filipinos. The overwhelming evidence for the superiority of using the student's primary language (Cummins 1994) which for many of the Filipino children may be one of the vernaculars cannot be ignored (Galang 1977). The success of educational programs in different countries in attaining the goal of bilingualism (Skutnabb-Kangas & Cummins 1988) provides support for the desirability of such a policy. The linguistic diversity of the country offers valuable linguistic resources that the Filipino people should be proud of and therefore should be enriched and preserved. Research on the amount of time needed for acquiring academically related competence in a second language could guide the choice of the media of instruction and the timeline for their introduction and use. Data suggest that at least five years is required for language minority students in the United States to approach grade norms in English language arts (Cummins 1994).

Rights affirmation is an important activity of language planning. A language policy that emphasizes language as resource not only recognizes the role of the different languages spoken in the country but also affirms the language rights of every Filipino and therefore provides for their use and development in the schools. Also, such a policy may help reshape attitudes toward languages and language groups and alleviate some of the "conflicts" emerging out of the language-as-problem and other orientations such as the opposition to the use of the national language and the tensions between the *Tagalog*-speakers and the non-*Tagalog* speakers, especially the Cebuanos.

When the languages spoken in the Philippines, both indigenous and non-indigenous, are considered as linguistic resources each playing an important role in the Philippine society, a more appropriate and acceptable bilingual education policy might be adopted. Such a policy could include provisions similar to the recommendations of the Congressional Commission on Education in 1991:

1. Use of the vernacular as the main teaching medium in the elementary school, especially in the early grades;

111

2. Introduction of *Filipino* and then English as subjects so that students can acquire and use them for social and academic purposes;

3. Gradual use of *Filipino* and later English as media of instruction, after students have acquired the necessary academically related competence in these languages; and

4. Opportunities for developing further the students' skills in the vernaculars, at least for those who wish to.

The resource orientation in language planning is not without challenges. Development is a necessary aspect of any resource-oriented policy. Considering the multilingual situation in the Philippines, a comprehensive plan for implementing such a policy needs to be developed by representatives from the different sectors of education and language groups. Such a plan might include specific language requirements at different levels, instructional materials in the different languages, and a national teacher training program.

NOTES

1. *Lingua franca* refers to "a language that is used for communication between different groups of people, each speaking a different language" (Richards, Platt & Weber 1985: 166).

2. *Vernacular* is the term used to refer to "a language or language variety in bilingual and multilingual countries spoken by some or most of the population but when it is not the official or the national language of a country" (Richards, Platt & Weber 1985:307). In the Philippines, this term refers to the indigenous languages spoken in the different regions of the country.

REFERENCES

Bautista, M. L. S. 1996. An Outline: The National Language and the Language of Instruction. In M. L. S. Bautista (Ed.), *Readings in Philippine Sociolinguistics*, pp. 223-227. Manila, Philippines: De La Salle University Press, Inc.

Beebe, J., & Beebe, M. 1981. The Filipinos: A Special Case. In C.A. Ferguson & S. B.Heath (Eds.), *Language in the U. S.* pp. 322-338. Cambridge, MA: Cambridge University Press.

Bernabe, E. J. F. 1987. *Language Policy Formulation, Programming, Implementation and Evaluation in Philippine Education.* Manila, Philippines: Linguistic Society of the Philippines.

Congressional Commission on Education. 1991. *Making Education Work: An Agenda for Reform.* Manila and Quezon City, Philippines: Congress of the Republic of the Philippines.

Cummins, J. 1994. Primary Language Instruction and the Education of Language Minority Students. In C. F. Leyba (Ed.). *Schooling and Language Minority Students: A Theoretical Framework* (2nd ed.), pp. 3-46. Los Angeles: Evaluation, Dissemination and Assessment Center, California State University, Los Angeles and California State Department of Education, Bilingual Education Office.

Davis, F. B. 1967. *Philippine Language-Teaching Experiments.* Quezon City, Philippines: Phoenix Publishing House.

Department of Education and Culture. 1974. *Implementing guidelines for the policy on bilingual education.* Department Order No. 25. Manila, Philippines.

Department of Education, Culture and Sports. 1987a. The 1987 *Policy on Bilingual Education.* Department Order Nos. 52 . Manila,

Philippines.

Department of Educaiton, Culture and Sports. 1987b. *Implementing Guidelines for the 1987 Policy in Bilingual Education.* Deparment Order No. 54. Manila, Philippines.

Galang, R. 1977. The Vernacular in the Classroom. In E. Pascasio (Ed.), *The Filipino Bilingual*, pp. 102-107. Quezon City, Philippines: Ateneo de Manila University Press.

Galang, R. 1988. The Language Situation of Filipino Americans. In S. L. McKay & S. C. Wong (Eds.), *Language Diversity: Problem or Resource?*, pp. 229-251. New York: Newbury House Publishers.

Gonzalez, A. B. 1980. *Language and Nationalism: The Philippine Experience Thus Far.* Quezon City, Philippines: Ateneo de Manila University Press.

Gonzalez, A. B, Ed. 1988. *The Role of English and its Maintenance in the Philippines.* Manila, Philippines: Solidaridad Publishing House.

Gonzalez, A. B. 1996a. Language and Nationalism in the Philippines: An Update. In M. L. S. Bautista (Ed.), *Readings in Philippine Sociolinguistics*, pp. 228-239. Manila, Philippines: De La Salle University Press, Inc.

Gonzalez, A. B. 1996b, Evaluating Bilingual Education in the Philippines: Towards a Multidimensional Model of Evaluation in Language Planning. In M. L. S. Bautista (Ed.), *Readings in Sociolinguistics*, pp. 327-340. Manila, Philippines: De La Salle University Press, Inc.

Gonzalez, A., & Sibayan, B. P. , Eds. 1988. *Evaluating Bilingual Education in the Philippines (1974-1985).* Manila, Philippines: Linguistic Society of the Philippines.

Guerrero, J. S. 1988. Medium of Instruction: Language Teaching Issue. *Philippine Journal of Education,* 103-104 and 142-143.

Juco, J. M. 1977. Bilingual Education under the New Constitution. In E. Pascasio (Ed.). *The Filipino Bilingual, pp.* 9-15. Quezon City, Philippines: Ateneo de Manila University Press.

Kaplan, R. B. 1982. The Language Situation in the Philippines. *The Linguistic Reporter,* 24 (5), 1-4.

Kelman, H. C. 1972. Language as an Aid and Barrier to Involvement in the National System. In J. A. Fishman (Ed.), *Advances in the Sociology of Language,Vol. II,* pp. 185-212 The Hague: Mouton.

Laygo, T. M. 1977. *What Is Filipino?* Berkeley, CA: Asian American Bilingual Center.

Llamzon, T. A. 1972. A New Approach to the Teaching of English in the Philippines. *RELC Journal,* 3, 30-39.

Llamzon, T. A. 1978. *Handbook of Philippine Language Groups.* Quezon City, Philippines: Ateneo de Manila University Press.

Mackey, W. F. 1979. Language Policy and Language Planning. *Journal of Communication, 29*(2), 48-53.

McFarland, C. D. 1996. Subgrouping and Number of Philippine Languages, or How Many Philippine Languages Are There? In M. L. S. Bautista (Ed.), *Readings in Philippine Sociolinguistics,* pp. 12-22. Manila, Philippines: De la Salle University Press, inc.

National Statistics Office. 1990. *Household Population by Mother Tongue, Sex, and Region.* Manila, Philippines.

Nolledo, J. N. 1992. *The 1987 Constitution of the Philippines.* Manila, Philippines: National Book Store, Inc.

Otanes, F. T. 1974. *Some Notes on the Educational Backgrounds of Immigrant Filipino Children*. Talk given to Operation Manong Volunteers, Honolulu, Hawaii.

Phelan, J. L. 1955. Philippine Linguistics and Spanish Missionaries: 1565-1700. *Mid-America*, 37 (13), 153-70.

Prator, C. H., Jr. 1950. *Language Teaching in the Philippines: A Report*. U.S. Educational Foundation in the Philippines.

Richards, J., Platt, J., & Weber, H. 1985. *Longman Dictionary of Applied Linguistics*. Essex, England: Longman Group Unlimited.

Ruiz, R. 1988. Orientations in Language Planning. In S. L. Mckay & S. C. Wong (Eds.), *Language Diversity: Problem or Resource?*, pp. 3-25. New York: Newbury House Publishers.

Sibayan, B. P. 1975. Survey of Language Use and Attitudes Towards Language in the Philippines. In S. Ohannessian, C.A. Ferguson, & E. C. Polome (Eds.), *Language Surveys in Developing Nations: Papers and reports on sociolinguistic surveys*, pp. 115-143. Arlington, VA: Center for Applied Linguistics.

Sibayan, B. P. 1996a. Bilingual Education in the Philippines: Strategy and Structure. In In M. L. S. Bautista (Ed.), *Readings in Sociolinguistics*, pp. 287-307. Manila, Philippines: De La Salle University Press, Inc.

Sibayan, B. P. 1996b. The Intellectualization of Filipino. In M.L.S. Bautista (Ed.), *Readings in Philippine Sociolinguistics*, pp. 240-253. Manila, Philippines: De la Salle University Press, Inc.

Sibayan, B. P., & Gonzalez, A. B. 1990. English Language Teaching in the Philippines: A Succession of Movements. In J. Britton, R. E. *pp. 269-298*. Clevedon, Avon: Multilingual Matters.

Skutnabb-Kangas, T., & Cummins, J. 1988. *Minority Education: From Shame to Struggle.* Philadelphia: Multilingual Matters.

Tauli, V. 1974. The Theory of Language Planning. In J. A. Fishman (Ed.), *Advances in Language Planning,* pp. 49-67. The Hague: Mouton. Shafer, & K. Watson (Eds.), *Teaching and Learning English Worldwide,*

AMAZING SPACE: REVIEWING THE ROLE OF CULTURAL ENVIRONMENT DEVELOPMENT TOWARD VALUES EDUCATION

Felice Prudente Sta. Maria

Molasses-coated banana chips that were a child's sticky joy to eat. Oil paintings of sun-bleached, palm-leaf houses and sunsets that ignited the sky. "Cows" called carabaos that liked bathing in mud. Beautiful Bayanihan Troupe folk dancers who never stopped smiling on their first world tour. And care-giving grandparents who spoke loving secrets in a melodious language without a single English word.

That was the Philippines while growing up off-campus near University of Southern California in Los Angeles, as father acquired another academic degree in the late 1950s.

Several years later, discovering the Philippines as home became reality.

One slept for the first time under a white, sheer, stiffly starched mosquito net tied to the four posters of an elaborately carved hardwood bed. The house had windows with opaque panes of oyster shell rather than clear glass. The bottom half of street-side walls slid open for ventilation and revealed florid metalwork that kept one from falling into the rainbow petals of frangipani boughs. On the garden's sunset side still stood the family's private pier with its arched trellis overtaken by fuchsia bougainvillea, and its stone wharf wading in the overflow of a canal clogged by pesky but lovely lavender waterlilies. Father's aunt said that a century ago, every home owned at least one boat which it decorated with buntings, fruits, and flowers to transport friends from one picnic, party, pilgrimage, and town fiesta to another. It was always a merry event accompanied by serenaders with guitars and flutes.

At that point in time, the memories of a lifetime one never had beckoned in every nook and shadow.

In the moonglow after a gentle May rain, a lady of the night vine bloomed. Its delicate white buds enraptured the bedroom with a heady fragrance that teased the imagination and made one wonder what secrets the riverine landing and the rest of the century-old ancestral home wished to reveal. As if on cue, the strains of a neighborhood piano drifted into the scene. It was playing a poignant melody called a *kundiman*—the ancient, native love song, so sad, so unquestionably straight from the heart, if not the soul.

How sensate is space. It is awakening and manifold. It imprints one's self-image with both heritage and transientness. It inspires. It insults. It implores. It is the memory of affection as fact.

Decoding Cultural Environments

Cultural spaces are aesthetic, economic, historic, informational, and symbolic in significance (Costin, 1991:27). If planned and managed for cultural development, they aid individual capability in self-assessment, self-expression and self-reform, thereby helping humankind discover its fundamental dignity (Girard, 1983:16). Cultural spaces may offer the cognitive theories of historical methodology, but they also can provide the affective stories with which a nation and its people sense their specialness, their singular saga, their continuing commitment to each other, the world, and their future. That nation-ness and nationalism are considered cultural artifacts (Anderson, 1995:4) is partly due to the conjuring power of cultural environments.

The amazing memorability of cultural space transmits tradition and demands discernment. Cultural sites include museums, paramuseums, libraries, historic sites and monuments, archives, libraries, performing arts venues, art galleries, alternative exhibition spaces, and culture zones. Memorials and shrines, sites of beginnings and endings, are sensory paradigms with both an endemic element demanding permanence, and an inherent insistence for contemporary interpretation and review. Just as religious sites and relics offer a spiritual catharsis and a transformation of wonderment, so are secular heritage properties affective springboards for awakening patriotism, courage, justice, humaneness, and all the values promoted by a country and a generation.

Valuing Values Education

Learning and culture symbiotically create and re-create. Andre Malraux defines culture as "the heritage of the quality of the world" (Malraux, 1956:632). Since its founding in 1992, the Philippines'

National Commission for Culture and Arts promotes culture in the Filipino national language as "the heritage of excellence and nobleness." Attention is on inspiring excellence *(kagalingan)* in skill, and nobleness *(karangalan)* of character. They are two considerations for establishing tangible and intangible indices of quality at stages of major socio-political change.

Periodically there are reassessments and redirections of lifestyles, social responsibilities, and environmental commitments. Values Education is a subject introduced into the Philippine elementary and secondary formal school curriculum in 1988. It was conceptualized to aid social transformation for building the "just and humane society" of an "independent and democratic nation" specified in the Philippine Constitution as revised in 1987. It was an age demanding economic reconstruction side by side with character reformation, after a fling with unwarranted authoritarianism. It was a period that prompted questioning by the Filipino people of their own integrity. Even Congress clamored for Moral Recovery.

The Values Education framework is descriptive rather than prescriptive, conceptual not exhaustive; it is broad and flexible. Fundamentally and intentionally culture-specific in its philosophy, Values Education seeks applicability in the social, spiritual, intellectual, moral, political, economic, physical, and social dimensions of the human person. It positions the self as a member of community. The subject identifies human dignity as the "supreme and overarching value that characterizes education."

According to Values Education, from human dignity flow seven core values, each with related values. The first four core values are: Health and Harmony with Nature (encompassing as related values: holistic health, cleanliness, physical fitness, reverence and respect for life, environmental care, beauty and art); Truth and Tolerance (love of truth, critical thinking, creativity, openness and respect for others, future orientation, scientific orientation); Love and Goodness (self worth or self-esteem, goodness, honesty/integrity, personal discipline, courage, trust, compassion or caring and sharing); Global Spirituality (faith in God, inner peace, religious tolerance, unity of all).

The remaining three are: Peace and Justice (respect and love for one's family, family solidarity, responsible parenthood, respect for human rights, concern for common good, cooperation, social responsibility and accountability, creative goodwill, fairness, appreciation of diversity, active non-violence); Sustainable Human Development (balance between economic and social development, protection of the environment, wise use of resources, responsible consumerism, productivity and quality, economic equity, work ethic, entrepreneurial spirit); Nationalism (love of country, heroism and appreciation of heroes and heroines, appreciation of cultural heritage, democracy, freedom and responsibility, civic consciousness and active participation, committed leadership, national unity) and Globalism (international understanding and solidarity, interdependence, appreciation of world heritage, cultural freedom, global peace).

A review of the original course description was undertaken in 1997, leading to slight revisions. They considered recommendations of the UNESCO International Commission on Education for the Twenty-first Century that had adopted four pillars for education: learning to know; learning to do; learning to be; and learning to live together (Delors, 1996:22-23). Values Education seeks to inspire inner transformation of the individual—an alteration in personal values and behavior. It is a welcome parallel to the "internal revolution" demanded by the secret society that promoted spiritual civics, while declaring the Philippine Revolution in 1896.

Values Education describes the idealized Filipino just as the Philippines celebrates the centennial of its proclamation of independence on June 12, 1998, and its inauguration as Asia's first constitutional democracy on January 23, 1999.

Clues in the Crannies

Culturescapes can carry in them "wishes of the nation" (Ishizawa and Endo, 1993:12). Five museums at historic shrines essential to the 1998 Centennial celebration were redesigned specifically as informal learning spaces for the subject Civics and Culture, required by basic education. Being institutionalized field trip destinations, the quintuplet provides a high-potential entry point for the character development desired by citizenship education.

At the heart of the cultural environment redevelopment philosophy is a discovery of the character-building values unquestionably present in historic events celebrated by each site, and identified by multisectoral dialogue as essential to the present and the future. At the core of the redevelopment methodology is the requirement that a *values-laden learning message must be a priority objective for each site's building design, exhibition curatorial plan, and overall project goal.* The message becomes a wish of the nation.

The five estates have site-specific learning messages in their storylines. But the stories string together in a continuous narrative. It reveals a history of national character that transcends customary focus on socio-political evolution and military intrepidity. In addition, the narrative relates to other historic sites where sculpture and plaques alone aid in awakening awareness of the complex interweaving that is any nation's former, current, and approaching diachronic life cycles.

Manipulation of the built-up environment subtly or eccentrically increases the amazing power of historic space. Space transforms into storyteller as it conserves period truthfulness in conjunction with contemporary critique and museology's multi-media. Whatever in a space might break its believability—the integrity of its values-laden story—is played down or removed. Historic site and theatrical stage set take on a similitude where every sense and intelligence must be catered to, if effective communication is to occur.

Setting the Stage

Perhaps the most amazing tribute to the Philippine Revolution, and the events it stimulated, is the home of Emilio Aguinaldo. He was an illustrious general who led rebel troops on November 11, 1896 into the revolution's first major victory, then catalyzed the proclamation of Philippine independence, the first Philippine congress, and inauguration of the Philippines as a constitutional republic two years and two months later.

Tradition supports that he redesigned his thatch-roofed ancestral home, in the 1920s, so no one would ever forget 1898. His two-story birthplace turned into a mansion that has been declared a Philippine National Treasure. Aguinaldo had to visualize a patriotic memory smothered by American Manifest Destiny—a belief held by the United States of America in 1898 that Philippine democracy was fraudulent and inconsequential, that Filipinos could not govern themselves, and that Yankee superiority must squire the birth of a real democracy side by side with establishing new export markets for products and services, as well as sourcing raw materials overseas.

The Filipino liberation army provided the land force that made America win the Spanish-American War in the Pacific quickly; but from 1899 till 1905, America waged war against its former ally. The "little war" predicted by Washington D.C.'s strategists resulted in costly horrors throughout the Philippines on the scale of Vietnam War's

Emilio Aguinaldo Shrine in Kawit, Cavite

MyLai tragedy. In 1901, Aguinaldo was captured and an American colonial regime that would last till 1946 was put into place. Filipinos were denied the truth: that they introduced democracy to themselves.

So Aguinaldo's architecture and interiors had to speak on behalf of the fallen and the silenced. A balcony supported by a native rendering of the faithful beast of burden, the carabao, became the center of attention every June 12—even if Filipinos had been reconditioned to celebrate July 4. On June 12, every year, aging veterans of the revolution turned up in their blue and white cotton cords to parade at the spot where the proclamation of independence took place. Heraldry of 1898 dominates the interior; ceilings and painted glass panels record historic vignettes. Finally in 1962, June 12 was declared the Philippine National Day.

Museum retooling teams, working on behalf of the 1998 Centennial, pledged to help Aguinaldo's message reach its audience. Replicas of blue and red satin curtains, as well as other patriotic period touches relegated to storage were added. Suddenly guests began discovering themselves immersed in a feeling for the Philippine flag, and an appreciation for the sacrifices made by Aguinaldo and his contemporaries on behalf of republicanism, and its potential for people's betterment. Aguinaldo's grand-daughter added her stories to the shrine's first portable audio-tour; it reveals an old-fashion lifestyle and a patriotic lifetime.

The ground-floor bowling alley was converted into a display of mixed memorabilia several years ago. Today, it is a museum devoted to the proclamation of Philippine independence. Its tale is told in contemporary fashion using vivid graphics, historical photos, historic documents, memorabilia, weaponry, timecharts, a repeating animated cartoon, a life-size hologram that dramatizes Aguinaldo on the eve of the proclamation of independence, and a video recreation of that special June 12 one hundred years ago.

Fort Santiago Shrine Honoring Jose P. Rizal

The four other historic spaces likewise infatuate, each flaunting a different appeal using period material, today's technology, contemporary verbal-visual language, and the power of space. Fort Santiago's shrine honoring Philippine National Hero Jose P. Rizal (1861-1896), during his last days prior to martyrdom before an imperial firing squad, is the only permanent Philippine exhibit in the minimalist mode. It is a tribute to a memory—a vital reminder that intellectual pursuit, creative flexibility, spiritual strength, a pure conscience, and humanitarian concern are national essentials for human development.

Two sparsely furnished second-floor galleries court introspection. One room infers mortality. Its centerpiece is a reliquary from Rizal's mother: a bone from his spine obviously grazed by a bullet. The second quiet space exhibits only Rizal's final laud to his homeland. Splendid parquetry tells his great grand-niece's version of how his family discovered the hidden verses inside an oil burner. At the far wall, etched end to end, is the entire valedictory work. A dramatic recitation of the poignantly stunning poem is just a push-button away.

Rizal's birthplace and site of exile also have been redesigned. The ancestral home is now dedicated to childhood and family's nurturing role. A recently installed, life-size bronze statue depicts the hero at age eight with a pet dog. That was in 1869, the year Spain acquired a constitution—an event that catalyzed political rethinking in the Philippine colony and Rizal's historic destiny.

Talisay barrio, where Rizal spent four years in forced seclusion, was indeed an abandoned part of the archipelago, although it had a Spanish military command and a Jesuit parish. Almost 50 years ago, the hero's former students contributed recollections towards governmental reconstruction of the estate with its clinic, hospice, school, orchard, farm, and home. Currently, the Centennial team is removing all elements of post-1896 intrusion from the hillside estate's interior space. Visitors will experience the semblance of a century ago from an innovative boardwalk that meanders around Rizal's personal space. All biographical data will be on the concrete route. The raised pathway was designed as non-intrusive to the remarkable natural setting with its towering trees, visiting monkeys, day crickets, and nocturnal wildlife. Information is to be set into non-corrosive metal which itself rests on sculptural forms meant to rust—almost as *memento morir*. Forever visible is the sea below—the escape route he refused to take, having given his word as a gentleman to the local commandant.

The fifth historic-site museum is an Asian treasure: a Roman Catholic church in Malolos, Bulacan that was converted temporarily into the Orient's first congressional session hall. Its convent uses multimedia to recreate events vital to fathoming the oldest democracy outside of Europe and the Americas. A timechart traces democracy's major characteristics—such as equality of all people, power coming from the people, all people being born free, majority rule, separation of church and state, and autonomy of local governments—back in Asia to the Philippine constitution of 1899. As the first civics education museum in the country, it promotes human rights side by side with corresponding responsibilities, and show democracy in action as it adapts to each milieu. A dropbox sends letters straight to the President and other political officers.

Fantasies and Feelings

One of the most ennobling definitions of liberty was made by Prime Minister Apolinario Mabini, a boot-strapping, physically challenged lawyer behind the first Philippine constitutional republic. He promoted liberty as the regained "freedom to do only good."

Among Filipinos, goodness and beauty are often interchanged, implying their non-dualistic character. For instance, Filipinos greet by saying *"Magandang umaga"* (Beautiful morning) rather than *"Mabuting umaga"* (Good morning). One's inner spirit is described commonly as *maganda* or *mabuti*.

Beauty is inseparable from the good feelings it stimulates. Memories are best kept alive by emotional attachment for them, thus the northern Philippine word *mailiw,* "remembering with affection." Native synonyms for memento—*maritata* in Filipino, *bunat* in Ilokano—have a caring and loving undertone. Similarly, the conservation of historic environments requires their association with good and beautiful feelings. If bereft of affectiveness and affection, tangible culture fails to stimulate remembrance of the national portrait—its fact and its fiction, its visions and its character-building values. If concerted image-making and identity-building are to stimulate feelings that build a sense of communal belonging and patriotic stewardship, they will require a touch of the fantasy wed to enthusiasm—the imagination that is aroused when the godly enters.

Inevitably, a people will seek their story, then tell and re-tell it in their own, convincing way.

They will be led to the actual settings where events occurred. They will hold in their hands relics of memory. And as they ponder their legacy of truths, they will discover the mythic dimension of their historic space and be glad that it can still amaze.

REFERENCES

Anderson, Benedict. 1995. *Imagined Communities: Reflections on the Origin and Spread of Nationalism.* London: Verson.

Costin, Cathy Lynn. 1991. Legal and Policy Issues in the Protection of Cultural Heritage in South Asia and the Pacific. In Margaret H. G. MacLean, ed., *Cultural Heritage in Asia and the Pacific: Conservation and Policy.* California: The Getty Conservation Institute.

Delors, Jacques, ed., 1996. *Learning: The Treasure Within.* Paris: UNESCO.

Girard, Augustin. 1983. *Cultural Development: Experiences and Policies. Paris:* UNESCO.

Ishizawa, Yoshiaki and Nobuo Endo. 1993. *Study on the Conservation of Monuments and Sites and Socio-Cultural Development: A New Methodology for Historic Site Engineering.* Tokyo: Institute of Asian Cultures, Sophia University.

Malraux, Andre. 1956. *The Voices of Silence: Man and His Art.* Stuart Gilbert, translator. New York: Doubleday and Company.

Philippine Centennial Commission. 1996. *The Handbook for Communicating the Philippine Centennial of 1998.* Metro Manila: Philippine Centennial Commission.

Committee for Education, UNESCO National Commission of the Philippines. 1997. *Values Education for the Filipino: 1997 Revised Version of the DECS Values Education Program.* Manila: Committee for Education, UNESCO National Commission of the Philippines.

1 0 0 Years
of Filipino
Presence
in America

{III}

THE FILIPINO DIASPORA AND THE CENTENARY OF THE PHILIPPINE REVOLUTION

E. San Juan, Jr.

Let us fight to our last breath in order to defend our sovereignty, our independence . . . Abject suicide will be the fate of anyone who will allow himself to be duped by the poisonous promises of the North Americans. For wherever we turn we are being pursued by race prejudice, which is deep, cruel, and implacable in the North American Anglo-Saxon.
    —Apolinario Mabini

Ang hindi lumingon sa pinanggalingan ay hindi makararating sa paroroonan. [One who doesn't look back to where he came from will not arrive at his destination.]
    —Folk aphorism

In August 1997, a National Filipino American Empowerment Conference was held at a time when few members of the community, much less the white majority, were heeding the cry for justice for thousands of Filipino World War II veterans denied welfare benefits. The timing was nicely ironic and self-incriminating. Meanwhile, as the centennial of the Philippine revolution approached, Filipino Americans congratulated themselves for the visibility of such "minority models" as Benjamin Cayetano, Jocelyn Enriquez, Tia Carrere, etc., oblivious of the cases of Flor Contemplacion, Sarah Balabagan, and thousands of Overseas Contract Workers (OCWs) in Hong Kong, Singapore, the Middle East, Europe, and elsewhere—this phenomenal Filipino diaspora born of post Cold War traumas has effectively projected Filipinos into the limelight as cheap domestic servants of the world. Despite this mutation of stereotypes, the fabled "mahogany-colored Manilamen of Louisiana" are still celebrated, together with the oft-invoked archaic pieties of *pakikisama* and *utang na loob*, as signs of ethnic primordiality (San Juan 1998). But if a diagnosis of these symptoms of anachronism and delayed reaction-formations is attempted, where should we begin?

The *fin-de-siecle* centennial of the Philippine revolution against Spain, and later against the United States, is one symptomatic touchstone for reflection on the plight of the bifurcated or dispersed national corpus. The official festivity began with a commemoration of the 1896 cry of Balintawak by the followers of the *Katipunan*, with Andres Bonifacio as its leading figure. It ended in June 1998, marking the 100-year anniversary of the founding of the Malolos Republic headed by General Emilio Aguinaldo. The first Philippine Republic of course did not last—on 4 February 1899, the Filipino-American War broke out, the revolution of the masses was cut short, aborted, only to erupt again several times throughout the American colonial period and the protracted neocolonial aftermath.[1] We are still living through an unfinished "permanent revolution" begun by our grandparents, a process still unfolding at the very moment we are asking ourselves, here in the metropolis several thousand miles away from Manila Bay where Admiral Dewey sank the Spanish fleet in May 1898, who is the authentic Filipino, what "truly or essentially represents the Filipino," how do we know we are Filipinos, and how can we be recognized for what we truly are by the majoritarian society.

Such questions may or may not have been put to rest, at best suspended, by the February 1986 "people power" revolt against the Marcos dictatorship and the subsequent removal of the U.S. military bases in 1992. In the perspective of the "long duration" of historiography, a hundred years is simply the wink of an eye, a pause in epochal cycles. Let us refresh our memory a little bit. In January 1900, Senator Albert Beveridge of Indiana intoned in the halls of Congress: "The Philippines are ours forever." Earlier, the distinguished philosopher William James wrote to a Boston newspaper: "It is horrible, simply horrible" as he bewailed the U.S. government's policy of "unspeakable meanness and ignominy" in the brutal suppression of the natives (Schirmer and Shalom 1987: 28; McWilliams 1973). That little-known "insurrection" triggered reverberations that produced historic effects far beyond the battlefields of Balangiga, Samar (the recent furor over the Balangiga bells is one more *déjà vu* symptom), or Tirad Pass in the Mountain Province.

Throughout Asia, from India to Malaysia and the China of Sun Yat-sen, our revolution against Spanish colonialism symbolized the awakening of dark-skinned peoples against Western domination. Rizal, for example, is highly esteemed not only by Indonesians, Malaysians, Japanese, and other Asians but also by millions of people in Latin America. When I visited Havana, Cuba, in the early eighties,

I found that Rizal's two novels (recently reissued) were best-sellers, probably read by more Cubans than Filipinos in the Philippines. In December 1997, I received an invitation to participate in a centennial gathering at the Casa de las Americas in Havana, Cuba, of representatives from countries whose fates were decided by the vicissitudes of the Spanish-American War at the turn of the century: Cuba, the Philippines, and Puerto Rico (one of the few remaining classic colonies in the world).

Needless to say, I am not a government factotum assigned to promote official celebrations, or essentialist apologetics. But since we are engaged in a process of critical reflection on our collective situation as "Filipinos" in the diaspora, there is reason for this review of the historical record. In the last few years, we have all been told that we should enjoy ethnic pride in the discovery that Filipinos arrived in the North American continent as early as 1587, at Morro Bay, California. Or that Filipino fugitives from the Spanish galleons settled in Louisiana in 1763, and so on. Now I am not against antiquarian research of this kind *per se*. It may provide leisure for some, a career for others. But surely there are other events we should invest in if our project is the vindication of our national/communal dignity, not just ethnic competition with Native Americans for precedence, and for democratic empowerment.

Like it or not, we surfaced in "Anglo" consciousness not as museum curiosities—one must say though, that the exhibition of Igorots, Moros and other "indigenous types" at the St. Louis Exposition of 1904 contributed to the fixation of a Filipino stereotype in the popular lore—but as a nation of resisters to U.S. colonial aggression and the power of U.S. imperial capital. If we want to change the stereotype, we need to change our orientation. Instead of acclaiming Gaspar Molina's part in building the first ship in California in 1720, why don't we acknowledge the achievements of Pablo Manlapit, Pedro Calosa, and others in organizing their compatriots in the Hawaiian sugar plantations in the twenties? Why not study the achievements of Silme Domingo, Gene Viernes, Philip Vera Cruz, and other dissidents during the long night of the Marcos dictatorship (Churchill 1995; Scharlin and Villanueva 1992)? Instead of opportunistically celebrating Wall Street brokers and idolizing successful businessmen and politicians like Ninoy Aquino now glorified in some murals of San Francisco and Los Angeles, why don't we pay attention to the struggles of so many unnamed Filipino nurses and ordinary employees in the sixties and seventies against discrimination and ostracism? And, likewise, those of domestics, "mail order" brides, and millions of OCWs scattered throughout the planet?

Choice of what events in the past to focus on indexes the kind of project we are involved in today. We select from the multiplicity of events in the past what can explain our present predicament and, by acting on its resonance, help us resolve it. The past is still alive and operating on us, whether we are aware of it or not. I suggest this point of departure for further inquiry. It is the invasion of the Philippines by the United States in 1898, the destruction of the revolutionary Philippine Republic, the annexation of the islands and the colonization of the inhabitants, that explains why we are all here in "the belly of the beast" (to use Jose Marti's phrase). Of course, why we (this "we" is still problematic) are all here (where, what social locations and imaginaries?) today is a more complex and vexatious topic than it seems, even though the history and sociology textbooks can provide the neat explanations about the institutional push-pull factors accounting for the third cohort of Filipino immigrants and particularly the post-1965 "waves" that have since become tidal indeed, making our "ethnic" community the largest of the Asian contingent—nearly 3 million, not including the TNTs, students, and other "birds of passage."

Perhaps I don't need to belabor what is common knowledge today: The anatomy and complexion of the majority of Filipinos in the United States today are profoundly different than those of the "Manongs" of Carlos Bulosan's time and of the veterans of World War II—240,000 of them, as you know, have never enjoyed full veteran's benefits; now, only about 70,000 are still alive waiting for the promised federal reward. According to the 1990 census, almost two thirds of Filipinos here (64.4%) were born in the Philippines. In most cases, the uprooted childhood and adolescence of many Filipinos here signify an experience whose crises and shocks of recognition, or joy of Americanization, as the case may be, are perhaps being registered now in the preoccupation with identity—who is more Filipino or less Filipino, who belongs and who doesn't. This partly accounts for the alienation currently registered in Asian American youth "gangs" as well as the anxiety of fetishizing the homeland. Whether you were born here or not, you are perceived by the dominant society as someone "alien," not quite "American," and somehow categorized as "Other." This is the inherent racial politics of the milieu we happen to inhabit.

As I have discussed in previous research projects, the narrative of the United States as a multiracial and multicultural polity is still in the process of being fought through; in the racial politics of that narrative, we are all implicated as protagonists (together with millions in the categorized groups) interrogating the hegemonic definition of "American" as centered in a patriarchal, property-oriented Western discourse opposed to the realization of a radically democratic, just, egalitarian order. But we cannot concentrate solely on what is happening within the territorial border of the United States; this border has tentacles extending to the Philippines, even though the military bases are gone (U.S. access, however, is guaranteed anytime by the Ramos regime [Schirmer 1977] and recently confirmed by the Estrada administration's approval of the Visiting Forces Agreement). For us Filipinos, that is impossible. You can ignore it, but it will not ignore you. Some of us are fascinated with the current idiom of "difference," hybridity, fluid and decentered personas or masks, transcultural subjectivity, syncretic and border cultures, and so on. But the process of globalizing via transnational corporations has not eliminated the power of the sovereign nation-state—you still have to get your passport, the U.S. military still flies its own flag (with the United Nations as sublimating agency) in Bosnia, Korea, and elsewhere, INS agents and border patrols still hunt for "undocumented" aliens. Witness how Germany and Japan (not to mention the old imperial rivals Britain and France) still consider Japanese or German as languages of prestige. In this post Cold War environment of interdependency, we are confronting what the ideologue of the bourgeois elite Samuel Huntington alleges as the "war of civilizations," a proxy for rivalry between the hegemonic industrial powers and the Islamic "rogue" or "terrorist" states (Sudan and Afghanistan, as of August 1998).

Let me cite here an example of a misleading diagnosis of our dilemma. Yen Le Espiritu, a Vietnamese scholar married to a Filipino, published sometime ago her research into the lives of Filipinos in San Diego entitled *Filipino American Lives* (1995). She concludes that Filipinos are now transitional or amphibious creatures sandwiched between assimilationist and pluralist paradigms, neither bipolar nor linear identities, cyborgs or denizens of a world in rapid metamorphosis. Clearly influenced by the precipitous mutations of the political economy of Europe in the nineties, Espiritu's thesis registers the postmodernist shift of sensibility. But the notion of strategies of cultural construction is not really anything new. Recall how the "Manongs" memorialized in Bulosan's *America Is in the Heart* devised ingenious ruses to circumvent racism and invent their own unique life-forms. In the late sixties, young Filipinos whose parents came after the War passed through the crucible of self-awareness or *conscientization* (to use Paulo Freire's term) in the turbulence of the civil-rights struggles, the youth "hippie" revolt, the antiwar movement, and the beginning of women's liberation. Now we are in a period of reaction, still at the height of the neoconservative "Contract with America" and the exorbitance of the "model minority" myth. Historical forces have problematized Espiritu's thesis: she failed to recognize the heavy, profound "colonization" of the Filipinos she interviewed because her utilitarian and empiricist framework assumed the legitimacy of the market system and unequal property relations, alienated labor as an unquestioned premise, the existing class hierarchy, and other liberal individualist norms underpinning the racial order. You certainly can't "read" the history and experience of Filipinos here and in the Philippines from the viewpoint of the oppressors and then claim universal validity for it. Today we need to ask in addition: Why is the "identity crisis" of the sixties acquiring a kind of "second coming" in the form of "identity politics" in the framework of the debate on *laissez-faire* multiculturalism? Why is the critique of "white supremacy" and institutional racism being replaced by managerial programs of cultural diversity and fundamentalist revivals harmonizing differences?

Lest some of you think I am imposing a personal agenda, I want to quote the formulation of many enlightened Filipino American students that these issues of identity, culture, community, history, and politics should be placed in "the context of movement and connection," in the context of multidimensional social changes. The aim is to promote dialogue, linkages, and unsettling of complacencies. Nothing is ever repeated exactly in the same form; what seems repetition is really a subtle metamorphosis that escapes our fixed habit of attention—a product of our socialization, self-administered "brainwashing." But since no system can guarantee its permanence, our struggle is not hopeless. So I propose a method of critique, not deconstruction (which, after so much noise, reproduces the same object or phenomenon unchanged), to reveal why our subaltern plight has worsened under the guise of self-help amelioration in this neoconservative moment. The paradox is epitomized, I think, by two recent events. What I say may offend tender sensibilities but this provocation, I think, is worthwhile if it can induce critical self-examination.

First, the Andrew Cunanan affair. Most of you know that before Cunanan's partial Filipino background was discovered, his identity was a mystery—his name sounded Irish, his appearance resembled a cross between a Latino and a Caucasian, indeed a "bastard" specimen. In the twenties, Filipinos almost escaped the antimiscegenation law when in 1931 the Court judged that we were not Mongolians; we belonged to the Malay group (some equated the Malay with the Mongolian—don't they look alike?). Because of this, the California legislature prohibited white-Filipino marriages, a law not repealed until 1948 (Chan 1991; Foster 1994).

When the facts about Cunanan came out, Filipinos in the Philippines felt so outraged that they protested in public that the nation should have nothing to do with Andrew nor with his father, a fugitive from justice hiding in the Philipines. In other words, they came out to disclaim Cunanan as Filipino. Alas, we would not even have the privilege of claiming our first highly publicized "serial killer," notorious only because his victim was a celebrity of the *haut bourgeoisie.* For students needing a topic for their thesis or research project, the life of Andrew Cunanan and the situation of thousands of Filipinos who lived and grew up in the shadow of the U.S.Navy present a challenge that can unravel the most crucial questions of racism, class divisions, homophobia, deception and chicanery in high society, and so on. Cunanan's trail is littered with the remains of our own colonial history that continue to haunt all of us, whether you are aware of it or not, whether you can "pass" or not. In our mediatized society governed by the mass consumption of simulacra and simulations of prestige, adventurers like Cunanan can be catapulted to become celebrity scapegoats that provide "canon fodder" also for hate-crimes and racially motivated genocide. Ethnic pride with the mark of vengeance, indeed.

Second, in the recent National Filipino American Empowerment Conference I mentioned at the outset, CEO Loida Nicolas-Lewis, the model-minority incarnate, pleaded on behalf of the unrecognized Filipino veterans whose fate betokens our own collective marginality. It was a symbolic gesture of solidarity. It was also a charitable act, and proof—according to *Asian Week* commentator Emil Guillermo (1997) —that Filipino egos can unite only when there is a victim who transcends our regional, class, generational, linguistic, and other divisions —all symptoms of our alleged "damaged" culture. This view of a charismatic figure required for ethnic unity presupposes the alienation and fragmentation that bedevils the structure of the "internal colonies" in the metropolis. Our neocolonial and subaltern condition has thus become endemic, respecting no borders or frontiers.

What is interesting, to my mind, is not this attempt of the petty politicians, what we call *trapos* back home, to exploit the case of the veterans for opportunist and careerist ends. So what else is new? Rather, it is the protests that erupted when a resolution was introduced concerning lesbian, gay, bisexual and transgender rights. Predictably enough, some aging patriarchs exploded in disgust—unequivocal evidence that for all its claim to being distinctive or singular, we reflect the antagonisms and contradictions of the larger society in which we find our lives tightly imbricated. Not only this, we reflect them in a parodic and grotesque manner since we tend to mimic the language and motions of the larger drama of U.S. society. We are often unaware of the fact that we have repressed our own histories and memories to serve our masters by following the rules of the game and pretending we have finally achieved parity if not equality with the guardians of white supremacy when we reproduce among ourselves the hierarchical power relations that assign us our position in society. This is not just servile mimicry but utter dispossession and self-disintegration.

What then (to echo a famous query) is to be done? Let me return to my original problematization of the two naively juxaposed terms: "Filipino" and "American." The project of empowerment of "Filipino Americans" cannot be launched unless we problematize that conjunction of two fields of subjectivity, two trajectories. It is easy to say that we are all citizens of the United States polity and also Filipino by ethnicity (this last is chiefly interpreted as descent, or blood lineage rather than cultural in the large sociopolitical signification). But mere juxtaposition does not clarify anything; in fact, it begs all the fundamental questions about autonomy, social justice, and equality in a society characterized by alienation and commodity-fetishism. This is starkly if pathetically exemplified by the following remark of Maria P. Root, the editor of a recent collection of essays entitled *Filipino Americans,* who states that she wants to be inclusive in her definition of the unhyphenated category—at last, free at last from the ubiquitous hyphen!

Root writes:

> *We are immigrants-now-citizens, American born, immigrant spouses awaiting eligibility for green cards, mixed-heritage Filipinos, students or workers on visa, tago ng tago (undocumented), and transnationals moving between the Philippines and the United States. Thus, Filipino American is a state of mind rather than of legality or geography. Under the same roof, family members hold different meanings for and attachments to being Filipino American. (1997: xiv)*

I want to underscore that telltale phrase "state of mind" for the benefit of any therapist or head-shrink in the audience. We ought always to beware of any call for us to set aside our differences because we are members of one family—the patriarch, to be sure, is brandishing the carrot while hiding the big stick. Political and historical realities cannot be so easily dissolved into individualist psychology without its effects haunting us no end.

Hopefully we are now suspicious of such psychological fixes and nostrums. One can sympathize with the urge to be ecumenical, to subsume everyone under the "same roof," to welcome everyone in the spirit of what the late Virgilio Enriquez (1992) once called *pakikipagkapwa*—his answer to what is authentically Filipino. This seems ideal provided of course everyone keeps quiet and continue to police their minds. Unfortunately minds don't simply float around in ethereal naivete; bodies and collision of bodies—the atomistic metaphor will catch up with us again—will remind us of the reality of lived experience, of our history as a subjugated and recalcitrant people, of the specific trajectories and genealogies of the terms "Filipino" and "American." This reality is contradictory and heterogenous, replete with inconsistencies and paradoxes. Just ask any Filipina "domestic" for further verification.

To be Filipino, or Filipino American, or just plain American—what's in a name? one might retort. Nothing much, perhaps, but then everything in certain circumstances. This is not just another semantic language-game, as everyone knows, in the context of court cases involving discrimination for speaking "Filipino" (or any of the vernaculars) in the workplace. Perhaps this may be rendered concrete if we cite the recent report that Hawaii Governor Benjamin Cayetano refused the label "Filipino American" when he was visiting the Philippines in 1995; the governor wanted to be labeled an "American" (Gaborro 1997) when he was in his parents' homeland. I wonder if the governor is aspiring for re-election by Filipino voters.

It may be suggested here that the simple explanation for the resort to metaphysics—it's just a "state of mind"—may be found in our historical amnesia. That is precisely the legacy of four hundred years of servitude, first to Spain, briefly to Japan, and up to now to the United States. The proverbial colonial mentality again, one might interject. This seems too easy. In the past, people simply threw at you Renato Constantino's books, if not those by Agoncillo, Abaya, and so on. But there's no alternative to doing critical analysis and research into the historical formation of Philippine society and the mentality of its constituent classes and sectors.

Our scholars are no help, either. Take, for example, the explanation by Linda Revilla and Pauline Agbayani-Siewert that Filipinos have problems here in the United States because of their "lack of strong ethnic identity." Filipinos lack cohesiveness because "they belong to numerous competing organizations based on dialects, regional origins, and kinship ties" (1995: 164). These inane tautologies and clichés may be found replicated in so many textbooks that you begin to wonder if academic study can ever save us from our fabled "native" indolence. But if this is the result of about a hundred years of "civilized" scholarship on Filipinos by American experts who are often cited everywhere—H. Brett Melendy, David Steinberg, Theodore Friend, Stanley Karnow, and so on—I'd rather choose the alleged "uncivilized" ways of the Aetas and Negritos. Beware of friends with a "civilizing mission"!

On the other hand, in talking about what distinguishes the Filipino, Revilla and Agbayani-Siewert repeat the same old Orientalizing traits: family togetherness, respect for elders, "smooth interpersonal relationships," and all the traditional values that distinguish a dependent and subjugated "Third World" culture, while at the same time claiming that "family authority is not patriarchal, but more egalitarian" (1995: 160). The last statement is definitely false. The paradigm that underlies this knowledge-production is the binary formula of tradition/modernity inscribed in the "Social Darwinist" discourse of evolution, hence Filipinos become acculturated or Westernized when they adopt non-ethnic values such as independence, individualism, assertiveness, and so on. And they begin to do this when they immigrate to the United States. Before the actual passage, however, they have already become assimilated, so to speak, because Philippine society is a replica of the imperial metropolis. Thus, despite the mechanical recitation of sociological banalities, our two scholars assert nonchalantly: "Filipinos are similar to most Americans in terms of language, customs, and values, and thus they are highly motivated to immigrate to the United States" (1995: 143). Lo and behold, in one stroke, all problems disappear. We are back to the position that it's all a matter of "a state of mind," a psychic disposition. Which doesn't hide the utter bankruptcy of almost all academic studies on Filipinos in the United States.

The reason why this is so I have already suggested earlier. The limitation of perspective inheres in the erasure of the foundational act of violence: United States colonial aggression, its destruction of the Filipino people's attempt (begun in 1896) to forge its own autonomous destiny, its continuing politico-economic influence on the Filipino ruling elite, and its cultural/ideological hegemony on most Filipinos. When you have occluded or dismissed this inaugural act that bound Filipino and American, the Philippines and the United States, then you can reduce all problems to a matter of ethnicity of beliefs, values, attitudes, and commonsensical ideas that (as the experts allege) have no grounding whatsoever in the social relations of production, in the complex nexus of material practices that produce and reproduce the lives of every Filipino in a particular geopolitical terrain. This of course is highly problematic. In this mode of thinking, the fundamental racial order of the U.S. social formation is obscured and replaced by a discourse of cultural differences and plural, even indeterminate, subject-positions. A mainstream version of multiculturalism capable of coopting protest and containing criticism now dictates the way we analyze every social and political event. By this reduction to superficial ethnic particularisms divorced from social needs and from the historical specificity of colonial bondage, alienation and reification—social conditions tied to the logic of the market and commodity-exchange—are reinforced. In this process, the matter of racism, not to speak of dehumanization by gender, class, and nationality, disappears *tout court* when it is sublimated into the peaceful or coercive management process of reconciliation and pacification of subject populations.

Before I conclude, I want to address the effect of the U.S. racial order on the public sphere of international cultural relations. I have in mind specifically how a certain pragmatic constructionism based on an implied social difference impinges on the way mainstream Eurocentric scholars, the agents of authoritative knowledge-production, respond to the attempts of Filipinos to articulate their own history of anticolonial revolution. I have performed critiques of such knowledge production in my previous works (1992; 1995). What I have in mind here is the recent attempt by Prof. Glenn May (1996) to debunk the heroic figure of Andres Bonifacio and castigate the Filipino historians and intellectuals who have (in May's opinion) conspired to foist the myth on a whole nation.

On the surface, May claims that he is not trying to attack the accomplishment of Bonifacio or his heroic stature; rather, he is trying to expose the shenanigans and hoaxes of such scholars as Epifanio de los Santos, Agoncillo, Ileto, and others. True enough, except that his doubts and suspicions as to the authenticity of the documents ascribed to Bonifacio, his reservations about the honesty and competence of the historians and scholars, and of course the gullibility of the Filipino public (not only the educated intelligentsia but the ordinary folk), accumulate a suasive force that not only the historiographical skills of certain individuals are questioned but also the moral character and integrity of Filipinos as a people. Such an entity as a "Filipino" interpretive community is constructed by May to serve as target for his polemics. If Filipinos such as the highly esteemed historians and intellectuals May accuses are wanting in integrity and honesty, then Bonifacio (and a host of other heroic figures) turns out to be a product of liars and forgers and deceivers. Such a blanket charge of mendacity begins to resonate so as to cast suspicion on the whole society as accomplices and accessories to the fraud.

Thanks to this conjuncture of events, we owe Prof. May this unsolicited service of setting us marching along the straight course of historical veracity and faithfulness to the truth. But is the professor himself a neutral value-free agent of empirical objectivity? Given May's methodological skepticism, we may express our doubt whether May's choice of investigating the life and works of Andres Bonifacio is chiefly a professional one, or is a systematic and deliberate program motivated by other than personal reasons. The conflicted relation between a neocolony and an imperial power can be dismissed by Prof. May, but it will not ignore him. So then we realize that the "special relation" of the Philippines and the United States that persisted smoothly through the Cold War period and survived the days of the February 1986 "people power" uprising, is being critically examined again in the midst of a resurgent revolutionary development (not just by the New People's Army but by popular forces cutting across class, ethnicity, religion, gender categories). This critique extends to the "interested" function of scholars like May and his ilk.

Following the lead of Filipinologists like David Steinberg, Peter Stanley, and Theodore Friend, Stanley Karnow, author of the best-seller *In Our Image*, began the counterrevolutionary strategy of explaining Philippine dependency as due to the failure of the U.S. colonial experiment. That is, the American colonial administration failed to change precapitalist Filipino habits, attitudes, norms—in order words, traditional Filipino culture endured and caused the underdevelopment of the society. We are responsible for our own misery, corruption, backwardness. Hence U.S. imperialism is not to be blamed for the ills of present-day Filipino society. May and like-minded experts follow in the wake of this apologia, this time imputing bias, incompetence, and plain ignorance to Filipino intellectuals and thus implying that such revolutionary heroes like Bonifacio, and more vulnerably Rizal, Mabini, and so on, can not really stand up to rigorous scholarly interrogation. What matters is not so much whether May has really proved his case, impugning the authority of Filipino historians; the damage has been done by innuendo, insinuation, polemical suspicion, and other rhetorical means of casting doubt on your enemy. What is primarily at stake is not historical truth but political advantage and global authority over the science of knowledge-production.[2] This has serious implications for the Filipino community here and its aspiration to affirm its autonomy and dignity.

Sometime last year I scandalized the gatekeepers at the University of California, Berkeley by my comment on the "ethnic cleansing" perpetrated by our putative allies. I denounced how Chinese and Japanese American professors hoodwinked Filipino students by pretending to be friends in their struggle for equity while stabbing them in the back. I warned that Filipinos should not trust other cohorts in Asian panethnicity because they privilege their own careerist interests and ethnocentric bias. What I really wanted to communicate was not this advice but a theme that I have already initiated in my earlier book *Racial Formation/Critical Transformation* and *The Philippine Temptation* and that I elaborate in my recent work, *From Exile to Diaspora*. This theme concerns the double and intrinsically dialectical trajectory of Filipino American history-in-the-making.

I sum up this theme in a provisional, open-ended way. The chief distinction of Filipinos from other Asians residing in the United States is that their country of origin was the object of violent colonization and unmitigated subjugation by monopoly capital. It is this foundational process, not the settling of Filipino fugitives in Louisiana or anywhere else, that establishes the limit and potential of the Filipino lifeworld here. Without understanding the complex process of colonial subjugation and the internalization of dependency, Filipinos will not be able to define their own specific historical trajectory here as a dual or bifurcated formation—one based on the continuing struggle of Filipinos for national liberation and popular democracy in the Philippines, and the other based on the exploitation and resistance of immigrants here (from the "Manongs" in Hawaii and the West Coast to the post-1965 "brain drain" and the present diaspora worldwide). These two distinct histories, while geographically separate, flow into each other and converge into a single multilayered narrative that needs to be articulated around the principles of national sovereignty, social justice, and equality. So far this has not been done because, as I have already pointed out, the orthodox textbook approaches distort both histories across the domains of experience characterized by class, gender, race, nationality, and so on. In the wake of the poststructuralist trend among intellectuals, a theory of Filipinos as transnational migrants or transmigrants has been introduced to befog the atmosphere already mired by the insistence on contingency, aporia, ambivalence, indeterminacy, disjunction, liminality, and so on. To avoid the "nihilism of despair or Utopia of progress," we are told to be transnational or translational, or else. But the notion of Filipinos as transnational subjects assumes that all nation-states are equal in power, status, and so on. Like assimilationism, this theory of transmigrants and transnationals obfuscates imperial domination and the imperative of rebellion. It reinforces the marginalization and dependency of "Third World" peoples. It erases what David Harvey calls historical "permanences" (1996: 347) and aggravates the Othering of people of color into racialized minorities—cheap labor for global corporations. It rejects their history of resistance and their agency for emancipating themselves from the laws of the market and its operational ideology of white supremacy.

Let me conclude by submitting this proposition for collective exploration: Filipinos in the United States possess their own historical trajectory, one with its own singular profile but always linked in a thousand ways to what is going on in the Philippines. To capture the contours of this trajectory, we need to avoid two pitfalls: first, the nostalgic essentialism that surfaces in the fetishism of folk festivals and other commodified cultural products that accompany tourist spectacles and official rituals. Tied to this is the cult of personality and the romanticizing of the indigenes. We need to connect folklore and such cultural practices to the conflicted lives of the Igorots, Moros, and masses of peasants and workers. Second, more dangerous perhaps, we should guard against minstrelsy, self-denial by mimicry, the anxiety of not becoming truly "Americanized," that is, defined by white-supremacist norms. I hope we don't want to be schizoid or ambidextrous performers forever, in the fashion of Bienvenido Santos' "you lovely people." This drive to assume a hybrid "postcolonial" identity, with all its exoticism and aura of originality, only reinforces the pluralist/liberal consensus of "rational choice theory" (the utilitarian model of means and ends that promotes alienation and atomistic individualism [Collier 1990]) and fosters institutional racism. On the other hand, the submerging of one's history into a panethnic Asian American movement or any other ethnic absolutism violates the integrity of the Filipino people's tradition of revolutionary struggle for autonomy, our outstanding contribution to humankind's narrative of the struggle for freedom from oppression by others and by brute matter.

Becoming Filipino then is a process of dialectical struggle, not a matter of wish-fulfillment or mental conjuring. For Filipinos to grasp who they are, more importantly what they can become—for humans, as Antonio Gramsci once said, can only be defined in terms of what they can become, in terms of possibilities that can be actualized in historical transformations—we need to examine again the actual circumstances that joined the trajectory of the Philippines and the United States, of Americans and Filipinos, constituting in the process the dialectical configuration we know as Filipino American in its collective or group dimension. The Filipino in the United States is thus a historical phenomenon understandable neither as Filipino alone nor American alone but as an articulation of the political, social, economic, and cultural forces of the two societies with their distinct but intersecting histories. We need to grasp the dialectics of imperial conquest and anticolonial revolution, the dynamics and totality of that interaction, as the key to all the questions we shall be wrestling now and in the next millenium.

NOTES

1. For an excellent analysis of the rise of U.S. imperialism and the dynamics of its political economy, see Jones (1970). For the historical details of the early contact between Aguinaldo and the U.S. government, the most informative account is by Sheridan (1900, reprinted 1970).

2. It is instructive to compare the way another American scholar, William Henry Scott, approaches the problem of historiographical accuracy in his comments on Guillermo Capadocia's version of the same events and figures he discusses in his monograph (1992: 75-76). The difference between Scott's and May's handling of analogous problems illustrates the antithesis between progressive and reactionary standpoints in international cultural relations.

REFERENCES

Agbayani-Siewert, Pauline and Linda Revilla. 1995. "Filipino Americans." In *Asian Americans.* Ed. Pyong Gap Min. Thousand Oaks, CA: Sage Publications.

Chan, Sucheng. 1991. *Asian Americans: An Interpretive History.* Boston: Twayne Publishers. Churchill, Thomas. 1995. *Triumph Over Marcos.* Seattle: Open Hand Publishing.

Collier, Andrew. 1990. *Socialist Reasoning: An Inquiry into the Political Philosophy of Scientific Socialism.* London: Pluto Press.

Enriquez, Virgilio. 1992. *From Colonial to Liberation Psychology: The Philippine Experience.* Quezon City: University of the Philippines.

Espiritu, Yen Le. 1995. *Filipino American Lives.* Philadelphia: Temple University Press.

Foster, Nellie. 1994. "Legal Status of Filipino Intermarriages in California. In *Asian Americans and the Law.* Ed. Chaney McLain. New York: Garland Publishing Inc.

Gaborro, Allen. 1997. "Essay on Filipino Americans." In *Akda-Philippine Literature.* <http://www.europa.com/~ria/essay.html>

Guillermo, Emil. 1997. "Smart and Serious." *Asian Week* (29 August): 5.

Harvey, David. 1996. *Justice, Nature and the Geography of Difference.* Cambridge, Mass: Blackwell Publishers.

Jones, Gareth Stedman. 1970. "The Specificity of US Imperialism." *New Left Review* 60 (March-April): 59-86.

May, Glenn Anthony. 1996. *Inventing a Hero.* Manila: New Day Press; Madison, WI: University of Wisconsin, Center for Southeast Asian Studies.

McWilliams, Carey. 1973. "The Philippine Temptation." *The Nation* (April 30): 548-49.

Root, Maria P.P. 1997. *Filipino Americans.* Thousand Oaks, CA: Sage Publications.

San Juan, E. 1992. *Racial Formations / Critical Transformations.* Atlantic Highlands: Humanities Press.

——-. 1995. *The Philippine Temptation.* Philadelphia: Temple University Press.

——-. 1998. *From Exile to Diaspora: Versions of the Filipino Experience in the United States.* Boulder, CO: Westview Press.

Scharlin, Craig and Lilia Villanueva. 1992. *Philip Vera Cruz: A Personal History of Filipino Immigrants and the Farmworkers Movement.* Los Angeles: UCLA Asian American Studies Center.

Schirmer, Daniel B. 1997. *Fidel Ramos-The Pentagon's Philippine Friend 1992-1997.* Durham, NC: Friends of the Filipino People.

Schirmer, Daniel B. and Stephen Shalom, eds. 1987. *The Philippines Reader.* Boston: South End Press.

Scott, William Henry. 1992. *The Union Obrera Democratica: First Filipino Labor Union.* Quezon City: New Day Publishers.

Sheridan, Richard Brinsley. 1970 [1900]. *The Filipino Martyrs.* Quezon City: Malaya Books.

THE *MANONGS:*
PAST AND PRESENT

Susan Evangelista

Seventy-five or so years ago, in the 1920s, when the Philippines was still an American colony, many of the more adventurous young men of the islands—the go-getters—gathered up their courage and sometimes their family's savings, and went to seek their fortunes in the United States. In his book *I Have Lived With the American People*, one early Filipino-American writer, Manuel Buaken, chronicles how it was that these young men were "lured" to America: in his own village, an early *balikbayan*, a Filipino who had gone to the U.S. and studied and returned home a doctor, came to talk in the town square one day, and Buaken, still a child, was all dressed up in his best *barong* to go and hear the man, the pride of the town, speak of the streets of America paved in gold. Of course the young men of the village wanted to follow him—and of course their families wanted to send them!

So off they went, literally by the thousands (there were perhaps 60,000 by 1930), to become part of the migrant farm cycle, moving up and down the coast of California and into Oregon and Washington, picking asparagus and lettuce and apples, and sometimes venturing as far north as the Alaskan salmon canneries, working as waiters in restaurants and "boys" in hotels during the winter when there were no crops to pick. They were called *Pinoys,* and later, when younger Filipinos arrived in the U.S., *Manongs,* and then eventually, *Old-Timers,* and although they have been maligned throughout their lives and afterwards, in different ways at different times, they remain pioneers, the historical "fathers" of present day Filipino-Americans, whether or not they acknowledge the debt.

History was not kind to these bright-eyed innocent young men: they were hit smack in the face by the Depression, and the unemployment and hard times that went with it, and by racial resentment and intolerance in the same anti-Asian California that had persecuted and sometimes murdered the Chinese who had built the railroads, and had made it illegal for the Japanese, the real innovators in California agriculture, to own land. It was not a good time to be an Asian in California. In contrast to the Chinese and Japanese who went before them, Filipinos had the indisputable legal right to enter the country (as citizens of a U.S. colony), but this same colonial status and the education that it entailed had given the Filipinos an idealistic sense of democracy, equal rights, and fair play, leaving them totally unprepared for the realities of racist California. In addition they had an irrepressible interest in white women, since so few Filipinas joined the migration, and these women found them utterly charming, which put them into even more trouble with the rough-necked men of the American Patriarchy.

Life was indeed hard. The work that the *Pinoys* did in the fields and in the canneries was rough, dirty, and dangerous—in the fields the stoop work was back-breaking, and in the canneries sometimes

160

fingers were lost to the sharp knives—and after work they gambled, drank, went to dance halls and Chinese pool halls that served free *chop suey* at midnight, sometimes fell in love, sometimes got into fights, sometimes went to jail. They did become political activists as well though—they were good organizers, and eventually started strikes in the lettuce fields and salmon canneries. They were verbal and communicative, writing, putting out newspapers, speaking out for the growing underside of U.S. society, the laboring classes, the immigrants.

Carlos Bulosan was of course the most famous of the *Manongs*: physically weak, Bulosan immigrated in 1930, spent two of the worst Depression years reading and studying and teaching himself to write in the Los Angeles Public Library, as a "warm, well-lighted place," and then became personally involved in labor organizing and in the journalistic back-up for the movement: he did the yearbooks, the newsletters, the letters to the editors of the town newspapers. One short scene from his famous chronicle of Filipino-American life, *America is in the Heart* functions as the turning point of the "autobiographical novel" and shows the *persona* in his sudden discovery of his own strength and power in his newly-matured writing skills: "They cannot silence me any more—I will tell the world what they have done to me!" he shouts out loud in his solitude, only slightly tipsy from the bottle of red wine he has emptied. And after that, of course, he goes on to do political writing and organizational work.

The short story "BE American" concerns itself with writing and political action: the narrator's cousin comes to town, a real *promdi* as we might say today, an innocent *provinciano*, a new arrival, full of ambition and naiveté. He wants to get a good education, so he buys himself expensive books which he is then unable to read. He wants to go to school, but working and studying at the same time exhausts him. He wants to become an American citizen, but he is told that that option is not legally available to Filipinos at that time. So he works, and works on, and is involved in a strike, and then in labor organizing—and then the narrator looses track of his cousin, except that every once in a while he receives a crate of oranges or a box of lettuce from somewhere where he knows the labor movement is active and his cousin is part of it, or he receives a news clipping of an editorial written by his cousin, or gets word that he has gone to jail for the cause. And in the end the narrator concludes that cousin Consorcio was a real American, a better American than citizenship ever could have made him, for he was struggling for the American ideal of equality and human rights for all. (Ah, a little sappy! Well, this has something to do with the way people wrote during those times—no one would dare to say such things now—but at least he admired the right sort of person!)

So these were the original *Pinoys*—they weren't yet *Old-Timers*—who struggled through the 20s and 30s. In 1941, the war broke out, changing everything both here and there. Some of the U.S. based Filipinos joined the military. Carlos Bulosan's brother Aurelio, for instance, joined an all-Filipino battalion set on liberating the home country, and they were indeed part of the landing in Lingayen and then in the Visayas. For those who didn't join the military, there were all sorts of new, war-related industries springing up, creating new jobs. Immigration was cut off for the time-being, stranding people like Bienvenido Santos in the U.S., as of course travel by sea would have been very risky. And when the war ended, the Philippines became independent, so the colonial relationship which had given Filipinos free entry into the U.S. no longer applied, and thus Filipinos then had to join the Asian quota system for green cards, which meant, in effect, that they couldn't go unless they had some special credentials, special educational status or professional skills.

And these changes isolated the *Pinoys* who at that point were gradually aging into *Old-Timers*.

The 60s brought the U.S. a new in-flux of Filipinos, who were young, talented, energetic—generally students, or people on cultural exchange programs. The incident on which Ben Santos centers his story "The Day the Dancers Came" is from this era, and therefore some attention to that story will show us how the image of the *Manong* had changed by that time.

The story is well-known. The dancers are modern young people from the Manila of the 60s—probably college students. They do Filipino folk dances, so we have to credit them with an admirable interest in their native culture. When they dance, they wear their native costumes, and you can just imagine the women with their long hair drawn back into buns—they'd probably have to quit the team if they cut their hair. They are no doubt a select team—perhaps the government is funding them and all their relatives are very proud—and they are on top of the world: a semester off to travel! Perhaps they are going to Europe too.

So there they are: Cultural Ambassadors.

Then on the other side we have Fil and his roommate Tony. The *Old-Timers*. They are two lonely old men, presumably retired by this time, simply living out their final days together. But their hearts are still in the Philippines. And Fil, when he hears the dancers are coming, is all excited: he will meet them, they are strangers and newcomers, and maybe they will feel like he did when he first arrived in the U.S. in the 20s. They will need guidance—he will take them around, any place they want to go, and they will be in awe of his command of the American scene, the way he knows where to go and how to do things in Chicago—and then, to top it off, he will cook Filipino food for them, and they will be amazed that he cooks so well, that he can find the ingredients he needs even in Chicago, that he has been able to preserve his own little corner of Filipino culture in this cold foreign city.

Tony, of course, knows better from the beginning. These kids have the world in their pockets, and they are internationalists, in the ways that students were internationalists in the sixties, educated, with unlimited opportunities, a different breed from the earlier immigrants altogether; what interest would they have in the lives of two lonely old men?

Tony's view prevails, as we probably know from the beginning it will. (That, of course, is not the drama of the story.) The students are polite, but they back away from Fil. They don't seem to see him or hear him. Worse still, they don't need him: they can function on their own, even here in his city, better than he can. Fil is the historical past of the Filipino in America—maybe the historical representative of the old colonial relationship—and the dancers no longer have any interest in this. Paradoxically this leaves Fil in the position where all he can do is try to record the present on his tape recorder—in other words, use one of the techniques of the historian to bring himself forward in time.

But as we see, that doesn't work either. So we are left with a very sad and pitiable old man, a representative of Filipino history, ignored and rejected by the new generation and unable to capture its spirit for himself. An image of the (irrelevant) past.

And so things stood in the 60s. But in the 70s something new and interesting happened: Asian Americans—which at first meant Chinese, Japanese, and Filipino-Americans—suddenly got very interested in their own history, in the experiences of their parents and grandparents, and in the literature that had been inspired by this history. They began pressuring universities to set up Asian American Studies programs, and they took new pride in their ethnic backgrounds. They stopped trying to be un-Asian, stopped hiding their Japanese grandmothers who were maybe picture-book brides and still couldn't speak English very well, stopped being ashamed of their Chinese fathers who were maybe illegals in the first place—TNTs— and had worked at the most menial of jobs. And when they started looking back to their early history and literature, what did they find? They found that Filipinos, even though they were the last group to arrive in the U.S., were the first group to start producing literary texts and historical documents in English! Of course we aren't too happy about all the historical antecedents of this situation, based as it was on colonial education, but in this instance it worked well, for truly the Filipino immigrant did better in becoming part of the United States than the other two groups, the Chinese and the Japanese, did, because they were conversant in English. And now they were in a good position to spearhead the Asian American Movement. And they did, for even today when Asian Americans start talking about their U.S. history, they turn first to Carlos Bulosan's *America is in the Heart.* The historians of the movement have had a field day digging through the old filing cabinets of Bulosan's cannery union in Seattle, unearthing documentation of the union, history-based stories, poems Bulosan wrote for fund drives. This stuff was all still there in the 70s—the union was still in its original building—and it had all been ignored while the men who wrote it (and lived it) were turning into *Old-Timers* like Tony and Fil.

So then we get a new movement and a new literature. We get people like the poet Al Robles who discovered that he loved sitting around bars and pool halls chatting with the last of the *Old-Timers*, probably in their late 60s by then, usually but not always retired, absolutely delighted that this burly, bearded young fellow—American grown but Filipino at heart—wanted to listen to their stories. Robles recorded hundreds of hours of such talk, and then decided that he had to know this history on a more experiential level, so he worked—went out into the fields and picked lettuce and hops, spent a summer in the Alaskan canneries, etc. Then he could write in the voice of the *Manong*.

Then he could write a poem like "Taxi Dance," in which he speaks in the voice of the *Manong*, in his youth, the grape-picker gone out dancing with "blondies," dance-hall girls who collect tickets from their partners, a ten-cent ticket for every three minutes of dancing, so that the poor *Pinoy* looses $5.00 in one night—that would seem like a lot of money then, but it felt good, it was pleasant, and a good escape. (In fairness to the "blondies," Robles has his *Pinoy* speaker say he thinks they only earn $2.00 a night—they are essentially workers too.)

Most contemporary Filipino-American writers, however, who were young people in the 70s, never really got into the world of the *Manong* young again, but knew him as an old man, maybe living in the famous International Hotel in San Francisco, stomping around Kearny Street—maybe like Fil in Chicago—but instead of representing him as an object of pity, they turn the *Pinoy* into a symbol of the history of struggle and oppression. So then we get poems like Prisco Tabios's "These are the Forgotten Manongs," in which he pictures the old men walking the streets, or sitting around in billiard halls, in which "the powerful scent of *bagoong*" has been thrown into the "melting pot of racism," and then he speaks of the men whose "labor, wit, and hope are documented on once a month social security checks." These are men truly forgotten by history: the only documents that attest to their struggles are their social security checks. But they have a history of their own—the "Goo Goo monkey" of course refers to some of the racist name-calling of another era—and this history, found now only in their dreams, will be told.

Then we have poems like Oscar Peñaranda's *Lakai* in which, again, the *Manongs* are old, but the poet sees and understands their history—Peñaranda, like Robles, actually tried out field work and cannery work, so he really would have some understanding of what it was like. And he talks about some of the grimmer aspects of the old men's lives—sleeping in theaters and going to girlie shows and whorehouses—but he also talks about sliming the "red pink silver chum king salmon" and picking grapes, and he ends with his admiration of these men and their history, saying, "I take my hat off, bow my head in shame for those who malign you." Maybe he realizes that some of those who malign the *Pinoys* are Filipino as well, like the members of the dance troupe who went to Chicago.

Finally I'd like to acquaint readers with a text which I think shows the Filipino American Movement in maturity, dealing with the last struggle of contemporary writers, which is quite simply how to incorporate the history of the *Old-Timers*, in all its pain and all its richness, into their own sense of identity. This text is also by Al Robles, and it is called *Looking for Ifugao Mountain*. Interestingly enough, it is a dual language book, although even the English version makes use of some Filipino vocabulary. The story starts when a young Filipino, named Kayumanggi but living in San Francisco, in Portsmouth Square in Chinatown, meets up with an *Old-Timer*, Tagatac, an old Ifugao man, and finds himself mesmerized by the old man's eyes. The sound of an Ifugao nose flute starts him off on a dream journey, hunting for his own basic Filipino identity. But he finds it isn't easily recovered: along the way he meets hostility and violence—a fisherman who tells him to just eat a little fish and go home, an angry farmer who orders him out of the field, a stampeding herd of carabao, some Ifugao warriors. Finally he meets a friendly Ifugao hunter who guides him through the rice terraces, invites him to share in a community banquet of roast pig, and then brings him face to face with the old Tagatac—and again he hears the nose flute. But at that point Kayumanggi finds himself back in Portsmouth Square, securely present in the here-and-now, in his own situation and his own life. He has learned that he can go back, but he can't stay; he can only live as himself. But he is acquainted with his "inner Filipino."

And that's the end of it. The *Manongs* are dying—even now there probably aren't many left—but when we stop to think about the history of the Filipino-Americans, and the literature that grew out of that history, we must take our hats off to the *Pinoys* who suffered through it all.

TEMPLE STREET: FILIPINO LIFE IN LOS ANGELES

Valorie Slaughter Bejarano

Temple Street, in the 1950s, was a warm and friendly neighborhood of families and shopkeepers, bustling in the post World War Two prosperity of Los Angeles. The war provided some changes for the better. Filipinos were able to slowly merge into the middle-class after years of discrimination. Citizenship was offered to young men who served in the armed forces. Filipina brides walked down the aisles of churches, dressed in embroidered gowns brought with them from their island homes. Antimiscegenation laws were dropped in California, making it legal for *Pinoys* to marry Whites (or anybody else they wanted). What had started as a bachelor society recruited to work the agricultural industry in Hawaii and California, became a close knit community that no longer had to hide from racist, anti-Asian sentiments.

Single apartments and run-down hotel rooms in Boyle Heights became homes with neatly tended yards and gardens from Virgil

Avenue to Beaudry Street, between Sunset Boulevard and Sixth Street. This is the world my father brought our family to in 1953. We were the "Flip" side of the coin, so to speak. He was an American who went to the Philippines after the war, and married my mom, much to the wrath of her *haciendero* father. They tried to start a life in his home state of Colorado, but encountered intense discrimination. Word of mouth, from other Filipinos who were "making it," led them to Temple Street, in Los Angeles.

Dad became a member of the Cebu Brotherhood and Mom joined the Sampaquita Women's Circle. Later in the decade, life would lead us away to many places, but they were all just circles that always led back to Temple Street. I think of myself as a Temple Street "brat." We lived in Angelino Heights. I went to Cortez Street Elementary School. My classmates were diverse, but with a growing Filipino presence. As families grew, siblings filled the classrooms. Everybody knew somebody else's big brother or little sister. Moms brought *pancit* to PTA potlucks and Dads coached little league teams.

We celebrated all together at the old Columban Church across the street from Belmont High School (which at the time was a totally cool place to go). It sat like a jeweled crown on top of Loma Drive. It had a bell tower, flagstone courtyards, fountains and statues. The song writing team of Lieber and Stoller went to Belmont. So did Jack Webb, the star of *Dragnet,* one of my favorite fifties TV shows. Filipinos were chosen cheerleaders, prom queens and sports heroes. They also filled the academic ranks, but that was not as important to me as rock and roll dance contests, beehive hairdos sprayed stiff with Aquanet and customized hot-rod cars, souped up and painted to cruise the neighborhoods from east LA to Chinatown and back again. In 1955 someone asked me what I wanted to be when I grew up and I remember saying with absolute certainty . . . "a teenager!"

Temple Street in the fifties was a cozy, safe place to live. People knew each other and stopped to talk often. Conversation dominated our lives, at the dinner table, over the backyard fence and on the phone. Telephones were commonplace in homes and TVs sprouted up in every living room.

Filipinos were proud consumers. They had good jobs, worked hard and bought on credit. Chevys, Plymouths and Dodges parked in driveways. I remember the year my Uncle Ted bought a used black Cadillac. Every weekend he made quite a show out of hand washing and polishing it. I held the hose, as he talked around the unlit cigar stub in his mouth, lecturing me on the importance of just the right kinds of soap and wax to use, as he worked forward in small circles.

Valorie Slaughter Bejarano as a young girl in Los Angeles California

Today's modern car wash can't provide the satisfaction I felt after working two hours with my uncle, rubbing and buffing every bit of paint and chrome.

I was an immigrant, but I was too young to know it. I grew up without an accent in an "English only" household. Disneyland opened and I was there in my Davey Crockett hat and saddle shoes. Most of the kids I knew had the same story: We were Americans. It wasn't until several years later that I realized that some of us were considered more American depending on the lightness of skin and hair. In the fifties we were Mouseketeers, hoola-hooping, popping gum and screaming for Elvis.

The era evolved with the times. The neighborhood changed and grew crowded with new comers, looking for different kinds of haven. People moved away and Old-Timers died off. The ones who set the standard for us all, grew old and quiet. Styles and values changed. The new immigrants were more educated and professional. They bought BMW's and Mercedes and moved to condos in the Marina and homes in housing tracts in Monterey Park and Carson. Temple Street became an inner city statistic and eventually a home for a new Art and activism. That's kind of ironic. It became what it always was.

Now, as a Grandmother, I return to Temple Street, wondering what I will tell my *Apo*. I will tell her the same thing I say to the university kids who come looking for someone to tell them about Dimasalang Christmas and when Columban church was built in an old fire house and the chapel was a converted horse barn. I'll tell them about Toning and Bobby Balbuena; he in his spats and cane and she in her picture frame hats and tightly corseted dresses. She wore too much makeup and he had a Clark Gable moustache. Together they were fabulous. I'll remember my Uncle Ted in his undershirt, watching wrestling in a darkened living room, lit only by the light of an eight inch black and white TV screen and the heady scent of my Auntie Feling's closet. I used to hide beneath the voluminous gowns of spangled chiffon and tulle ternos, that held traces of Chanel and Dior.

Years ago developers demolished most of Bunker Hill. From downtown, they bulldozed west and called it progress. Now construction is going on to build the new Belmont Learning Complex. I hear the old Belmont will become a middle school. I passed the construction site not long ago. It was swarming with workers and dirt moving trucks. On Beaudry and Court Street, a cluster of Victorian houses once crossed in a maze above Temple Street. One of them was Uncle Ted and Auntie Feling's first home. Searching back through memory, I try to picture it. It's hard. There are no more familiar markers left.

Uncle Ted Sarno's Filipino band in Los Angeles, mid–1950's

For those who want to know what it was like, I give you this: A cookie cutter Victorian with a wide porch and a creaky screen door that always slammed shut. There were stairs you climbed up to a little elevated lawn with neatly trimmed grass. Gardenia bushes nestled against the house and honeysuckle and jasmine climbed the trellis that mounted the porch stairs. In the evenings, when Uncle Ted was at work, Auntie Feling loved to bang out "I'm in the Mood for Love" on their upright piano accompanied by the dulcet tones of her dog, Kitsie. I sat on the glider on the veranda watching the night turn the eucalyptus trees black. The warm summer air was heavy and muffled the sounds of traffic winding its way home. Dogs barked and kids ran down the street laughing, while their Mamas hollered them home. The old heavy glass and iron lampposts came on and old folks went in for the evening. Downtown, sparkled in the darkness.

FOLKLORE AND CREATIVE AGING AMONG ELDERLY FILIPINOS IN LOS ANGELES

Susan N. Montepio

The elderly have always played an important part in the field data collection of folklorists who regard them as repositories and transmitters of tradition. Folklorists have relied on the knowledge and wisdom that the elderly have accumulated through the years, recording their songs, narratives, beliefs, and practices. However, there are very few studies about the individuals themselves, who they are, what they do. This trend sadly implies that the elderly are more attuned to the past than to the present and that they spend the remaining days of their lives reminiscing and passing on, rather than actively creating, tradition. In recent years, as folklorists have shifted their attention from folklore items to the process of creating tradition, they have come to realize that the elderly are more than mere repositories. Studies show that the elderly are still capable of creating folk art and are just like other people in their creativity and use of expressive forms and communicative processes.[1] Contrary to popular belief, the elderly have not lost the ability to cope with advancing age and are still capable of reviving as well as creating folk traditions.[2] They not only keep traditions alive, they have found creative ways of using these traditions as a resource for coping with the present and its challenges and problems.[3]

The relative lack of studies on the aged and the process of aging is not confined to folkloristics. Anthropology, which like folkloristics looks on the elderly as a rich source of field data, is also guilty of this neglect in spite of its proponents' interest in the study of the life cycle. Anthropologists all over the world have studied pregnancy, childrearing practices, and growing up, but rarely have they written more than a paragraph or two on growing old. The ethnographic study of elderly Jews by Barbara Myerhoff[4] and of Filipinos by Rene Somera[5] are noteworthy exceptions. Myerhoff's book, *Number Our Days,* is an ethnographic study of a group of elderly immigrants from Eastern Europe who utilize the services and facilities of the Aliyah Senior Citizens Center in Venice, California. Myerhoff asserts that the elderly, contrary to popular belief, can remain in full command of the basic human faculties of insight and imagination until the very end. Somera, in *Bordered Aging,* presents an ethnographic study of daily life in a Filipino home for the aged. Somera notes that in the Philippines where it is a cultural tradition for families to care for their own elders, a home for the aged is a relatively new social institution which generally caters to the "socially and economically disadvantaged older people."

This paper is based on a study of a group of elderly Filipino immigrants in Norwalk, California and their use of folklore as a creative adaptation to both their aging and ethnic status. Folklore as used in this paper includes those categories and processes of traditional and expressive behaviors, such as rituals and celebrations, foodways, narratives and narrating, beliefs and believing. I see folklore not only as traditional items passed on from generation to generation, but also as an active and ongoing process, being created, modified and perpetuated in the present. I use the term creative aging to refer to the way the elderly in my study are creating, modifying, and perpetuating traditions as a resource for coping with the process of aging and the challenges and problems that come with it. I believe that the stories people tell, the metaphors and symbols they use, the food they prepare and share, the rituals they perform, and the way they dress can provide information about their values and concerns. People often tell stories, for example, about what concerns them most, and their values are implied in their reactions to the behaviors of other members of the organization and the events that take place around them. What individuals believe in and value are instrumental in shaping their attitudes and behavior. All the elderly in my study are active members of the

Filipino Senior Citizens in Norwalk, California

International Seniors Club of Southern California (ISC), a voluntary organization of individuals at least 55 years of age. I am interested in the role played by this organization in the lives of its members, especially in relation to the process of adaptation to their elderly and ethnic status. I believe the Club has succeeded in providing its members with a sense of identity, belonging, and purpose. It has, in fact, taken over some of the social and cultural functions of the family. Family members are always invited and usually attend the group's celebrations, thereby providing a chance for the "erring" family members to assuage feelings of guilt and neglect and in the process mend the chasm created by the change in their life style as a result of immigration and incorporation into American society with its entirely different culture and values. Through well-planned organizational activities, the group tries to forge a link to the past by engaging in traditional rituals and celebrations.

The elderly in my study do not at all fit the stereotype of helpless individuals who have lost the ability to cope with advancing age. On the contrary, they are actively and creatively living what can be considered a "good and meaningful life." Most of them have come to the United States upon the request of their children, not only to keep the family together but also to help take care of the grandchildren. In the Philippines, growing old means staying home and being cared for by younger members of the family. The elderly expect to be served and nurtured by their children and grandchildren in return for the sacrifices they had made through the years. This expectation is premised on the Filipino cultural value of *utang na loob* [debt of gratitude] which permeates all aspects of the Filipino's interpersonal relationships. *Utang na loob* is incurred when an individual accepts help from another. The person helped has an obligation to return the favor, and most often, this debt is never fully paid so that the feeling of gratitude, accompanied by the need to return the favor, sometimes lasts forever.[6]

The elderly in my study spent their early years in the Philippines under American rule. They had been educated in a system patterned after the American public school system and brought up to believe that immigration to America, the "Land of Promise," is synonymous to success. They are at a stage of their lives wherein they expect to lie back and enjoy the fruits of the sacrifices they had made in raising their now "successful" children. When they arrived in the United States; however, they were confronted with an entirely different culture, failed expectations, and diminished support network. They found themselves in a situation where the values are very different from what they are used to and their answers and solutions to everyday questions and problems are not always applicable to their present situations. It is like trying to learn lessons all over and younger members of the family who have preceded them in the United States are now more knowledgeable than they are. What results is a reversal of roles where children try to teach their parents the "acceptable" way of doing things in the American culture. Such a situation is not always taken favorably and usually results in culture clash within Filipino American families.

One of the first things that the elderly immigrants learned is that life in the United States is very different from that in the Philippines and one of the most dramatic differences is the rhythm of everyday life. They have been used to a slow and leisurely way of doing things, but now they see their children frantically trying to do more than they have time for. Most of the elderly I interviewed complained about being left alone in the house and their consequent lack of mobility because their children do not have the time to keep them company or to drive them around. In the Philippines they would have drivers, either one of the relatives or hired help, to take them wherever and whenever they want to. If they do not have a car, public transportation is very accessible, or if they live in a small town, everything is within walking distance and all the residents are either relatives or friends. Even if all their children are working, very seldom would the elderly be left alone in the house. There would always be either a member of the extended family, or a maid to keep them company, or they could go visit a neighbor and play cards or gossip. Coming to America did not only plunge them into an unknown and foreign land, it also "imprisoned" them because of their inability to move freely from one place to another without the help of somebody who can drive. They were helplessly lonely because of the absence of extended family support and the children whom they came to be with are too busy wrestling with their own demons. They were confused because their expectations of their elderly role conflicted with reality. Traditionally, they would be content to stay home and enjoy the leisurely life of the elderly. However, a big part of that traditional enjoyment has been wrenched from their environment. In contrast to their life in the Philippines where they were surrounded by family and friends, they suddenly found themselves all alone in a strange place.

The family and kin group that used to shower the elderly with attention in the Philippines are too busy trying to earn a living in the United States. This situation has been very difficult, not only on the elderly themselves, but on their family as well. The elderly are lonely and feel alienated from their children. On the other hand, the children are bewildered and frustrated over their parents' seemingly unreasonable demands for attention. Fortunately for most of the elderly I interviewed, their past experience of being able to take control of their lives has helped in the way they have decided to break free from their traditional role and take whatever the present has to offer, and in the process reinvent their lives so that their remaining days would be happy and meaningful.

Instrumental in this major change in their lives is their membership in the International Seniors Club of Southern California. Although the organization was initially envisioned as a multi-ethnic group, its membership has remained predominantly Filipino. The International Seniors Club provides a setting in which the elderly can speak their language, celebrate, feel important, and most especially, make and develop lifelong friendships. Their use of the senior citizens center exemplifies the kind of compromise they had to make. In the Philippines, they relied on their family, relatives, friends and neighbors to fulfill their needs for socialization. Here in the United States, their traditional support system is eroded by their children's desire for material success, and by the Pacific Ocean separating them from their long-time friends. Thus, they felt the need to establish meaningful relationships with non-kin. They tried to turn to their neighbors, who in the Philippines were part of the extended network of support. Unfortunately, they discovered soon enough that their neighbors were generally of the same age as their children with the same concerns and most often, nobody was home during the day. When they did find people of their age group in the community, linguistic and cultural differences often hampered the establishment of close relationships with non-Filipinos. Through well-planned organizational activities, the International Seniors Club has succeeded in forging a link to the past by deliberately bringing in traditional rituals and celebrations, dancing, dressing, food and other categories of symbolic and expressive behaviors. They took these traditional genres and modified them to fit into their present lives. Where they could not find something to use, they created their own rituals and celebrations, and perpetuated their own traditions. These rituals and celebrations provide the elderly with a vehicle for self and collective presentation, thus minimizing their feeling of isolation, invisibility and liminality. Individually and as a group, they have retained a distinctive culture that exhibits both continuities with the traditional way of life in the Philippines and new forms and modes of cultural expression which have arisen as a result of the experience of immigrating, resettling in and adapting to a new land, and responding to and adopting aspects of American culture.

One of the most popular activities among members of the International Seniors Club is dancing. They perform folk dances during special occasions but they prefer modern dances during their weekly get-togethers, as well as during monthly socials and special events. Since men are outnumbered, the ladies dance with each other, in pairs, in groups, or they line dance. Through these events, the International Seniors Club has successfully realized its goal of providing its members with "wholesome and worthwhile recreation." The members also look on dancing as an activity that can cure their physical ailments. As one of them said:

> *By dancing we release our stresses. Dancing exercises our bodies, stimulates circulation, and we sweat out cholesterol and lower our blood pressure to normal levels. Dancing makes us vigorous and cheerful and it helps alleviate our aches and pains. It is a source of great delight to us.*

The women are always well-dressed during all Club activities. Most of the time they are actually over-dressed. They use modern gowns or preferably, traditional Filipina dresses during most of their special events. It is very interesting to note that some of these women had never owned or used a traditional dress in the Philippines but in the United States they all have *ternos, kimonas,* and *Maria Claras,* three of the most popular and elegant of Philippine dresses. The elegance of these traditional dresses has become an effective means of ethnic display and is a constant source of ethnic pride.

Two of the most important club activities, the *Santacruzan* and the beauty pageants, have become the most elaborate means for the elderly to present themselves and their culture. The *Santacruzan* or *Flores de Mayo* [May Festival of Flowers], is the most popular of Philippine festivals. In the Philippines, it is the culmination of a month long devotion to the Virgin Mary. Here, the religious part is lost and it has become a secular event culminating in a parade of "beauties," and characters based on the Philippine *Santacruzan.* The *Santacruzan* gives everybody a chance to participate and wear their elegant dresses.

Filipinos participating in Santacruzan event

Beauty pageants are as important to Filipinos in the United States as they are in the Philippines. Once a year, ISC members choose a Ms. Philippines and her court, Ms. Luzon, Ms. Visayas, and Ms. Mindanao—just as they do in the Philippines. Candidates sell tickets and whoever sells the most wins the coveted title. Some of the candidates spend thousands of dollars. The family usually gets involved in selling tickets to get their mothers/grandmothers chosen, so the coronation becomes a well-attended family affair. Participation in these activities becomes both a vehicle for social interaction and a means of self expression as well as collective presentation. Other Club celebrations include Christmas, New Year, Valentine's Day, Easter, Mothers/Fathers Day, Philippine American Friendship Day, Halloween, and all other Filipino and American calendrical events. Using both the Filipino and American calendar of events provides them with more than enough holidays to celebrate. When they run out of holidays, they use their creativity and imagination to come up with fun themes for their parties. They especially celebrate the individual—they choose a muse for every club event, they recognize Golden Jubilee couples (those married for fifty years and more), Mother/Father of the Year, and birthday and wedding anniversary celebrants, thus giving people the attention that they feel they don't get enough from their children.

I also observed a lot of examples of narratives and narrating among the elderly in my study. They are very fond of reminiscing and storytelling, eager to be heard from, eager to relate parts of their life history. They tell their stories to whoever would listen. Their stories are not only devoted to marking their successes or unusual merits; rather, the stories are efforts at ordering, sorting, explaining—rendering coherent their long life, finding integrating ideas and characteristics that help them know themselves as the same person over time, despite great ruptures and shifts. Their immigrant experience and the loss of their original culture make them even more prone to seek continuity and coherence. Often these stories are idealized and sentimentalized, preserving what has been lost, and restoring it to life by incorporating it into the present. In talking about past experiences, individuals remember those events and activities that have influenced their growth and development as well as their present beliefs, values and concerns. The "old person reintegrates that past identity in the present, projecting it as part of his or her present self-image."[7]

The feeling of severe invisibility and the consequent disturbing psychological and social consequences of being unnoticed propelled these individuals to devise ways of presenting themselves to the world; of interpreting the meaning of their history and culture to a wider outside world that would remember them after they had died. Fortunately, they were able to reverse this invisibility. Through their own ingenuity, imagination, and feisty spirit, they succeeded in reinventing themselves, and in the process make their life more exciting and fun. By refusing to accept the invisibility and isolation, they made themselves seen, and in being seen they came into being in their own terms, as authors of themselves, creating an entire culture of their own making by creatively adapting old cultural traditions to fit a new set of circumstances. By so doing, they proved that they are not just repositories of tradition, but vigorous makers of culture. They have not actually replaced the old way of life with a new one. The old survives by rising to the new demand, by adapting and intensifying. In a society where everything does not always make sense, they have learned to compromise by incorporating old behavior patterns into a new system and vice versa, making it possible for them to continue to live actively and productively through the remaining days of their lives. When they remember and talk about their past experiences, they do not do so for the sole purpose of basking in past glories or accomplishments. Rather, they are using these past experiences as an effective resource in their present lives and circumstances. The skills developed and the wisdom honed through the years come in handy as they respond to failed expectations and the challenges of a new environment. The legendary strength of character and passionate love for freedom that made possible the 1898 Revolution against Spain and the 1986 People Power Revolution against Marcos live on in the hearts of my elderly informants as they fight for their right to live life to the fullest.

NOTES

1. Studies that look into creativity and the elderly include Alan Jabbour, "Some Thoughts from a Folk Cultural Perspective," *Perspectives on Aging: Exploding the Myth,* edited by Priscilla Johnston (Cambridge: Ballinger Publishing Company, 1981); Bess Lomax Hawes, "Folk Arts and the Elderly," *Festival of American Folklife Program Book,* edited by Thomas Vennum (Washington, D.C.: Smithsonian Institution, 1984); Simon Bronner, *Chain Carvers: Old Men Crafting Meaning* (Lexington: The University Press of Kentucky, 1985); and Roberta Cogan Krell, "Folklore and the Elderly: Aging, Creativity, and Community." Dissertation, Ph.D. in Folklore and Mythology, University of California, Los Angeles, 1986.

2. Mary Hufford, Marjorie Hunt, and Steven Zeitlin, *The Grand Generation: Memory, Mastery, Legacy* (Washington, D.C.: Smithsonian Institution, 1987).

3. Patrick B. Mullen, *Listening to Old Voices: Folklore, Life Stories, and the Elderly* (Urbana and Chicago: University of Illinois Press, 1992)

4. Barbara Myerhoff, *Number Our Days* New York: Simon and Schuster, 1978. Also see Barbara Myerhoff, *Remembered Lives: The Work of Ritual, Storytelling, and Growing Older* (Ann Arbor: University of Michigan Press, 1992).

5. Rene D. Somera, *Bordered Aging* (Manila, Philippines: De La Salle University Press, 1997).

6. Tomas D. Andres, *Dictionary of Filipino Culture and Values* (Quezon City, Philippines: Giraffe Books, 1994).

7. Mullen, *Listening to Old Voices,* p. 18.

100 Years
of Filipino Literature
(Oral and Written)

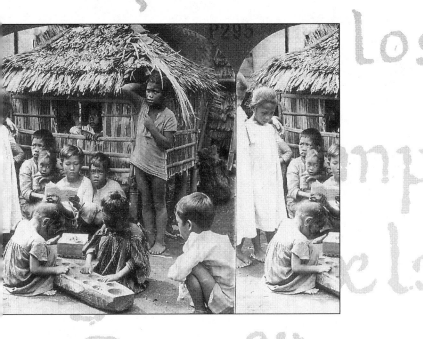

{IV}

THE TAUSUG BALLAD
OF PUTLI ISARA:
COLONIALISM,
RELIGION AND GENDER

Herminia Meñez

The centenary of Philippine independence from Spain, along with the revolution against the United States immediately following, is an appropriate time to examine the colonial experience as depicted in oral literature. In a recent analysis of that experience in nine Philippine novels, Jaime An Lim (1993:xiii) points out that despite the centrality of colonialism in the nation's history and culture, it has not been a central theme in literary criticism. The same is true in folklore studies.

The colonial regimes under Spain (1521-1898) and the United States (1898-1946) have had a profound impact on Philippine literature and folklore. One of the most important colonial legacies is the introduction of Euro-American literary models and, consequently, the relegation of native oral traditions to a marginal position vis-a-vis written literature and literary criticism. In recent years, however, efforts to develop a national literature have emphasized the need for contemporary writers to connect with the rich and largely untapped oral traditions of indigenous communities.

Oral literature, as this analysis points out, is a complex verbal art that also is culturally resonant. The ballad of Putli Isara[1] from the Tausug of Sulu is not only an artistic piece; it encapsulates crucial themes in Philippine history. Over the domestic focus on the relationships between lovers, parent and child, husband and wife, brother and sister, arches the larger theme of the colonial encounter. Colonialism also magnifies the issues of religion, race and gender, and personal martyrdom becomes a religious and political resistance to colonial oppression. Throughout history, the Tausug have resisted to the death the imposition of Christianity on Muslim subjects, which was at the heart of the Spanish conquest of Mindanao and Sulu.

The ballad is set in Jolo, capital of the Sulu archipelago, a chain of coral and volcanic islands extending from Zamboanga to the Malay state of Sabah in Borneo. The Tausug, the dominant ethnic group in Sulu, have been Muslims since at least the end of the 14th century, and today consider themselves the premier defenders of Islam in the southern Philippines. Through two colonial occupations by Spain and the United States, as well as during the Japanese occupation of the Philippines in World War II, the Tausug fought for independence as an Islamic state. In alliance with the Maranao and the Maguindanao, also Muslims, they repulsed colonial forces from the late 16th century until 1876 when the Spanish navy surrounded Jolo and burned down the seat of the Tausug sultanate (Majul 1973, Majul 1985).

The ensuing Spanish occupation of Jolo in the late nineteenth century provides the historical background of the ballad. *The liangkit parang sabil,* roughly translated as the ballad of ritual suicide, typically is a memorial to religious-political martyrdom. Not only is the *parang sabil* a religious act; so is the performance of the *liangkit*. The heroes are exclusively male to reflect the fact that only men in real life could mount a *jihad,* i.e., an attack against infidels or Christians (Rixhon in Abdul 1973:160; Kiefer 1970:6).[2] In 1899, when the United States took control of the Spanish garrison in Jolo, the capital had been walled to ward off these attacks by the *sabil* or *mujahid,* male warriors who killed and died in the path of God. In that culture of protected womanhood, women were, and still are, excluded from attaining the highest honor of dying "an innocent death" that would merit a direct journey to paradise on the back of a flaming white horse (Rixhon in Abdul 1973:160).

The ballad of Isara, performed by Indah Annura, a popular female singer from Jolo, is therefore unique in that it glorifies women warriors—Isara and her mother, Matagpis. They attack the Spanish garrison in Jolo to avenge personal honor, but ultimately to defend the most important religious and cultural values. Although Isara's fiance fights and dies with her, and her little brother attempts to avenge her death, the song reveals the failure of the Tausug patriarchy—as represented by Isara's father—to defend Islamic traditions against foreign hegemony.

The ballad opens with a reference to the Spanish occupation of Jolo which frames the tragedy foreshadowed at the start:

Let me tell you
About the Spaniards
While they lived here
They caused great turmoil (verse 1).
At the same time it was prophesied
That two lovers would commit suicide (verse 3).

The cataclysmic impact on the lives of the colonized is rendered not in a straight forward chronicle of events but in dramatic scenes. The plot unfolds in a series of ironic twists, adroitly employed by Indah Annura to build tension in the narrative. In the opening stanzas, Putli Isara, daughter of a *panglima*, a district chief, and her fiance, the handsome Abdulla, seem to be happy while preparing for their wedding. From the beginning, however, Isara's brilliant beauty causes problems: few men can resist her sexual appeal. Because of strict religious taboos against sexual contact, the physical attraction between the two lovers causes unrelieved emotional tension.

Isara was beautiful
And had a shapely body.
Whenever her fiance would look at her
She would soon run leaping (verse 9).
While running to her room
She would shout.
Even oaths of doom she would utter (verse 10)

According to Islamic *adat,* custom, the slightest touch between lovers is prohibited, for as one proverb puts it, "A man and a woman [together] are like gasoline and a match; they will burst into flame." Or, as another proverb which places the onus on women points out "Man cannot remain an ember when woman has more fire" (Hassan 1973:222). Images of fire persist throughout the ballad. Isara's behavior in the presence of her fiance betrays the raging flame within her "shapely body," although it is masked by her madonna-like countenance, her "angel-like beauty." As she herself points out to her father, "Try to consider/The probable consequences when two lovers are together" (verse 22).

Partly to dampen their ardor, the dutiful Abdulla leaves for a foreign land to purchase wedding gifts as part of the customary bride price. Ironically, however, in his absence, Isara's sexual attractiveness becomes even more dangerous. She decides to bathe in the river, despite her father's warning about sexual predators in the wilderness. She defies his orders to remain in seclusion while her fiance is away because in her own words, "I have too much grime/That I cannot sleep" (verse 26). Her decision, as the ballad audience would soon see, results in a grime no water can wash away.

Isara's tragedy stems also from what the singer interprets as a flaw in her character. It is her willfulness—"an undesirable trait"—that puts her in conflict with her father. At the river, the rebellious Isara refuses to depart in haste when her little brother warns her about the arrival of the Spanish soldiers. She stays long enough for the moment that would alter forever her fate and that of all the others in the story.

In this highly-charged scene, the meeting between man and woman turns into an encounter between colonizer and colonized, oppressor and oppressed. The confrontation between a white, male, Christian, foreign soldier and a brown, female Muslim native highlights the religious, sexual and racial conflict, but the status of Isara as a colonial subject plays an even stronger role in its outcome. Further, Isara discovers that her upper-class status as the daughter of a district chief does not grant her any privilege in the eyes of one who holds himself above the law and tradition of the conquered land. Soon after she invokes her elite position, she realizes her subjugation. Although Fundamentalist Islam and nineteenth century Spanish Catholicism held similar sexual taboos, in the lieutenant's mind, Isara does not merit the respect reserved for women of his race and social background. Even when she warns him that she is engaged to Abdulla, he replies in arrogance:

"Dear, even if you are engaged
You will be my partner.
Abdulla might be enraged
[But[I will just shoot him later." (verse 41)

Whether or not rape occurs is left to the imagination of the audience. But, no matter how Isara's phrase, "a soldier touched my body," is interpreted, the conqueror's mark can be obliterated only by a *jihad*.

When Abdulla returns from Sandakan bearing sweet-scented powder and expensive silk for his bride, he learns about his fiancée's disgrace. This scene, as before, makes use of contrast and irony to underscore the instability of life as colonial subjects. In the midst of what appears to be a blissful reunion of the lovers—while Abdulla seductively describes his gifts—Isara thinks of ways to break the tragic news. But once known, the two act fast. A wedding is out of the question as they instead arm themselves for an attack against the Spanish headquarters.

In the yard of the garrison, both Abdulla and Isara are active combatants. The singer, however, focuses on Isara as a *mujahid*, a male warrior. Like him, Isara carries a *barung*, a knife with a single-edged, leaf-shaped blade—a symbol of Tausug manhood. Like her male counterpart, she is "insane with rage," a "deadly hacker." Without warning, she thrusts her own weapon into the chest of her oppressor and seducer.

"Here is my barung [she tells him]
Feel it on your body
For your undesirable act" (verse 86).

In the next lines, Indah Annura does not spare the audience the violent scenes associated with the *liangkit parang sabil*. The words, "hacking," "in rage," and "bathed in blood" are formulaic; but ballad formulas are not just technical aids in oral composition; they are artistic devices that effectively evoke memories of similar performances. The listener, in this case, can juxtapose other renderings of a *mujahid* with the following portrait of a female combatant:

The beautiful Isara
Was very swift in hacking
When the guns sounded
In rage she shouted (verse 97).
All of a sudden
He was bathed in blood (verse 104).

Having carried out her oath, Isara disappears from the battle scene and is replaced by another warrior woman—her mother Matagpis. Defying the stereotype of submissive wives, Matagpis possesses a courage superior to that of her daughter. She berates her husband's loss of manhood, the native word of which, *usug*, also implies sexual potency. The *panglima* has refused to avenge his daughter's death in the hands of infidels. He refuses to listen to the message sent, through a boy, from the Spanish headquarters to pick up Isara's corpse so that the family can prepare it for burial in accordance with religious practice. He tells his wife:

"Just leave [her] there
She disobeyed my counsel (verse 120).
I will never pick [her] up
Whatever is the problem,
That is up to you [to solve] (verse 122).

The resolute Matagpis then heads for the garrison, a lone woman against hundreds of men, a sword against rifles and cannons.

In a deftly-crafted scene, the singer transforms an ordinary housewife into a *mujahid* by using the same ballad formulas, just mentioned, and which are typically applied to the male warrior:

[Matagpis] jumped up and raged
As she raised her kris (verse 140).
She hacked left and right.
The mother was crazy with anger.
The Spanish soldiers
Were running like hell (verse 142)
The captain said,
"We should retreat
She is as bold as the devil
No bullet can reach her" (verse 147).

When Matagpis finally falls in a rain of bullets, a mare takes her up to paradise to join Isara and Abdulla, who in death are "nosed" together by one flaming white horse to the sky. Having fought to the death their Christian enemies and colonial oppressors, the three attain martyrdom. In a typical *liangkit parang sabil*, the text should end here with the formulaic closure, "And then she died" (verse 151), which also appears, for instance, in Kiefer 1970:18, line 332: "And then they were killed," and in Tuban 1977:156, verse 129: "They all died without wounds/Only their bones were broken."

The ballad extolling the *jihad* of Putli Isara and Matagpis in the defense of Islam underscores not only the aggressive stance of the Tausug against colonial domination and Christian conversion. It subverts the traditional imagery of women and the concept of heroism as the exclusive right and privilege of men. Further, it also reveals the failure of the Tausug patriarchy at a critical time when a political leader's duties to Islam and the Islamic state should take precedence over personal matters (see Majul 1985:68, for a contemporary parallel).

Political reorganization during the Spanish regime, and thereafter, seriously threatened the power of political leaders like the *panglima* who ruled their respective districts. The same was true during the American occupation. Contrary to the ballad's depiction of Isara's father, however, it was not the norm for wealthy patriarchs, including district chiefs, to compromise their religion and politics in order to preserve their social status. In fact, another *liangkit parang sabil,* set in the American regime, provides a dramatic contrast to the ballad of Putli Isara. It glorifies a true-to-life hero, Panglima Hassan, who led a band of warriors against American military forces in the battle of Bud Datu on March 4, 1904 (Tuban 1977:138-156).

In the eyes of Matagpis, her husband has failed not only as a father to Isara but as a defender of Islam. His refusal "to take the path of God," to avenge his daughter's honor and to retrieve her corpse indicates that he has accomodated to the Spanish presence; at the least, he fears reprisal for the women's attacks on the fort. Moreover, he also fails as a father to his only son. He tries to dissuade him without success from taking up the cause of the women, because, as he puts it: "We have nothing to worry about/For we have plenty of money" (verse 156). Ironically, in the end, there is no family to protect or provide for, no son to perpetuate the lineage, for the boy has sworn to avenge the women, and to bring back his sister's corpse.

After saying his prayers and shouting his farewell, the *panglima's* son attacks the garrison and kills four soldiers. Upon seeing the boy, the lieutenant orders the men to stop firing. Instead of hanging him, a Spanish officer adopts the child, for in his words:

"When he grows up and matures
He might be of help to us (verse 168)
The boy in the future
May be able to soften the heart [of the people]" (verse 169).

The objective of the Spanish conquest of Mindanao and Sulu was to subdue the so-called "Moros" in order to eliminate Islam from the Philippines just as Spain had dealt with the Moors in her southern provinces. Isara's brother, under the tutelage of his adoptive Spanish parent, becomes the emissary of that colonial enterprise. The boy's adoption by a Spanish soldier and his role as a prospective mediator suggest a possible compromise solution to the religious-political conflict, a solution which appears acceptable to the adopted son:

The shrewd captain [said],
"Yes, very well, then
You are now my son,"
"Yes, very well then,
It is already understood.
I am now your child,
And you are now my father" (verse 176).

As in any complex piece of literature, written or oral, the ballad of Putli Isara offers a wide range of ambiguous and even conflicting meanings. The coda recounting the boy's *parang sabil* which ends with his adoption and his assumption of the role of Spain's emissary contravenes the focal point of the ballad—the women's *jihad*. Although the coda may seem to be simply an addendum to the ballad of Isara, the singer apparently intends this complication to express the complex, ambivalent relationships between colonizer and colonized.

From the start, Indah Annura casts the boy in the role of messenger and adviser, a role foreshadowed by a young native courier sent by the Spaniards to Isara's father. Early in the story, Isara's brother cautions his sister about the impending disaster and admonishes her to depart from the river. Later, the prescient boy at the time of his mother's death at the camp has a vision of her astride a mare. He even predicts his own death. Before leaving for the fort, he warns his father, "After I shall have said my prayer/My grave will be the headquarters" (verse 163). But the coda proves that his prediction is wrong. He does not envision his conscription as Spain's agent to his own people. The final irony is that the same brother who warned the heroine about the arrival of Spanish soldiers would in the end betray the cause of his mother and sister.

Some of these ambiguities, ironies and contradictions, which the singer unveils in her complex depiction of colonialism's impact on native societies, find resonance in the recent history and politics of Mindanao and Sulu (Nur Misuari in Majul 1985: 134-142). As is commonly known, the war for independence of Muslim Mindanao and Sulu did not end with the two colonial regimes, but even intensified during martial law under the dictatorship of President Ferdinand Marcos. On February 7, 1974, approximately a hundred years after the fall of Jolo to Spanish naval forces, Sulu's capital was razed to the ground in a violent encounter between the national army, navy and marines and the Moro National Liberation Front (MNLF). Nearly a quarter of a century of fighting has passed since that fateful defeat. However, throughout those years, and as recently as 1995, violent encounters between government forces and militant Islamic groups, especially the Abu Sayaff (Turner 1995:1-19) regularly took place in parts of Mindanao and Sulu. In September 1996, the national government and the MNLF signed a peace agreement that ended the MNLF-led rebellion in Mindanao, but as one observer has described the preceding negotiations "fear and renewed warfare rather than genuine tolerance forms the basis of current peace initiatives" (Sales 1996:56, 62-63). Despite the establishment of an autonomous region of Muslim Mindanao (ARMM), with Nur Misuari, the former leader of the MNLF, as the first governor, for the most dedicated rebels, the warrior ethos survives.

These wars also have affected women's consciousness. Like the men they believe in the political and religious basis of the war for an independent Islamic state. Tausug gender politics, however, still revolves around traditional bifurcated roles of the active, public man and the passive, private woman. Whereas a boy's public life intensifies at puberty in conjunction with his preparation for his role as a warrior and defender of Islam, a girl who starts to menstruate withdraws from the company of boys and men who are not her relatives. She remains in seclusion until marriage while learning domestic skills. Marriage, not warfare, is her prime destiny (Moore 1981).

In "Women and Warriors: Defending Islam in the Southern Philippines," Ruth Laura Perry Moore points out that, in contrast to the men, women view their role in the defense of Islam as future brides, wives and mothers of warriors. It is in these capacities that they embody, preserve and transmit religious and cultural values. For that reason, Tausug women, as the embodiment of their society's highest ideals, make it worthwhile for their men to fight and die for Islam. That is the ethnographic reality as the anthropologist describes it. However, she neither cites Indah Annura's Putli Isara, nor does she chart, as the ballad does, the possibilities for willful, fearless women in a patriarchal society to be like the heroine and her mother—active, independent agents of their own destinies.

If "it is in our literature that we recover our history" (Linda Ty-Casper in Lim 1993:xiii), oral tradition likewise certainly deserves a central place in our review of the Philippine experience during the past century. Looking back one hundred years and beyond, we can unearth artistic gems like the ballad of Putli Isara—rich not only in sociopolitical and cultural history, but in themes and imagery about women, which all contemporary writers of literature, feminist and otherwise, can connect with in their own imaginings as we journey forward, a hundred years and beyond.

NOTES

1. "The Parang Sabil of Abdulla and Putli Isara" is one of the best pieces in the repertoire of Indah Annura (Rixhon, 1973:160). The text in Tausug and English consists of 184 verses. Each verse consists of 4-6 rhyming lines.

2. According to Kiefer (1970:6), who uses the term "ritual suicide" for *parang sabil,* its major purpose was not to kill but be killed by an evil person so that one could merit a privileged afterlife. According to Rixhon (1973:160), however, *parang sabil* has been "strongly discouraged by most Sulu leaders, for the cause of *jihad* or holy war in the defense of Islam was often absent in most of the instances it was committed." It is therefore important today for militant Muslims like the members of the Abu Sayaff to proclaim their war against the military as a *jihad* (Turner, 1995).

REFERENCES

Abdul, Mohammad Daud, Rose Marie Adjawe and Ricardo Adjawie, translators. 1973. The Parang Sabil of Abdulla and Putli' Isara in Spanish Times. *Sulu Studies* 2:160-191. Introduction by Gerard Rixhon.

Hassan, Irene & T. Iklali Jainal. 1973. A selection of Tausug Riddles and Proverbs. *Sulu Studies* 2:210-232. Kiefer, Thomas. 1970. *Langkit Parrang Sabbil kan Apud. Music from the Tausug of Sulu, Moslems of the Southern Philippines: Recordings, notes and photographs.* New York: Anthology Record and Tape Corporation.

Majul, Cesar Adib. 1973. *Muslims in the Philippines.* Quezon City: University of the Philippines Press.

— 1985. The *Contemporary Muslim Movement in the Philippines..* Berkeley: Mizan Press.

Moore, Ruth Laura Perry. 1981. "Women and Warriors: Defending Islam in the Southern Philippines." Ph.D. diss., University of California, San Diego.

Sales, Peter. 1996. War and peace in the Southern Philippines: An Analysis of the Negotiations Between the Ramos administration and the Moro National Liberation Front. *Pilipinas* 27: 56-63.

Tuban, Rita. 1977. *Tausug Folk Literature.* M.A. thesis, University of the Philippines.

Turner, Mark. 1995. Terrorism and Secession in the Southern Philippines: The Rise of the Abu Sayaff. *Contemporary Southeast Asia* 17:1-19.

VIBRANT, VULGAR, VIGILANT: A HISTORY OF THE FILIPINO NEWSPAPER

Ruel S. De Vera

At first glance, it seemed like a perfect match, recently elected Philippine President Joseph Ejercito Estrada, the colorful actor-turned-politician, and the media establishment which was fascinated with his every move. But within weeks of his term, Estrada was already trading barbs with reporters, saying they guessed at government issues, just for circulation's sake, and that they make a living out of criticizing others.[1] He wouldn't sit down for a proper press conference with Malacañang (the presidential palace) reporters and while he had a testy relationship with the media in general, he singled-out one newspaper, the *Philippine Daily Inquirer* (the broadsheet this writer works for) as peddling lies about renovations to the presidential guesthouse.[2]

Yet in many ways, the media created Estrada, and the newspapers gave him more coverage than any other candidate during the recent elections.[3] Estrada himself asked the media to give him a chance.

While every Philippine president has had a love-hate relationship with journalists, it has been more so with Estrada, with his professed dislike for "ambush" interviews and, well, the *Inquirer*. It is a relationship that epitomizes the important role played by, as well as the liabilities that come with, Philippine newspapers, the freest press in the only democracy in Asia.

Vibrant, vulgar, and vigilant, Philippine newspapers exemplify many of the traits that make the Filipinos unique, while crafting an intensely fascinating story all their own. They have witnessed revolutions both bloody and bloodless, seen the rise of orators and dictators. Theirs is a story that mirrors the Filipinos' search for freedom as well as the obstacles they continue to encounter as part of free, powerful growth.

Past Tense

The rich history of newspapers in the Philippines gives some clue to the abundant promise and problems that they face today. In a country with a rich oral tradition, newspapers began their rise during the over 300-year rule of the Spaniards. The fires of the Filipino uprising against Spain would also fan a defiant spirit that would grow more evident in the later years. While magazines such as the *Philippine Free Press* and the Tagalog language *Liwayway* would have their own impact, the newspapers were first to emerge and gain lasting influence over a miniscule reading public composed mainly of the elite, specially in their years of infancy. A chronicle of those years can be gleaned from Crispin Maslog's *The Metro Manila Press*. Though no record of more than a single issue could be found, the publication of the newsletter *Succesos Felices* in 1637 is an achievement in itself. It was a time of compromise and simmering discontent under the Spanish. It would be in 1811 that the first regular serial, the *Del*

Superior Govierno came out. Like *Succesos Felices,* the *Superior* carried only foreign news and lasted only 15 issues. The first daily, the *La Esperanza,* began in 1846 and was followed by several other dailies, chief of which was the *Diario de Manila,* which would go on for 38 years, and the *El Comercio,* which lasted 56. Despite heavy censorship among other issues, not all the first newspapers were afraid, as can be judged by the political thinking of *La Opinion,* which criticized the Friars.[4] These were the highlights of the first dailies, which pioneered print journalism in a country of limited literacy. Furthermore, these newspapers were in Spanish because the rulers did not want the Filipinos to learn to read. That would change, and so would the news-papers.

The revolution against Spain of the late 19th century, which saw the birth of the military group KKK, gave birth to fiercely political papers, missives with missions. Most prominent of these was the Spain-based *La Solidaridad,* edited by Graciano Lopez Jaena, and boasting of the work of some of the Philippines' sharpest minds like Jose Rizal and Marcelo H. del Pilar, among others. Banned, and debated about, the *Soli* nonetheless spoke of political reform but its being written in Spanish limited its circulation. Still, the furor it raised demonstrated the power of the printed word. The single issue of the Katipunan's underground *Kalayaan* was enough to incite the masses, as it was written in Tagalog. As hostilities continued under American rule, newspapers such as the *La Independencia* and the *El Renacimiento* kept up the fight against the colonizers. While the American takeover is supposed to have instituted press freedom, strict libel laws stunted its growth. Most of the papers were obviously pro-American, but by the time the pro-Filipino *Philippines Herald* was founded, two future greats were already around. The original *Manila Times* was the first English language daily set up in 1898 and would go through several incarnations, but eventually reached prominence despite being closed down temporarily in 1930. The *Manila Bulletin* was founded in 1900 as a shipping newspaper but would go on as well to unprecedented longevity.[5]

The Second World War shut down the newspapers, but the liberation of Manila brought out a whole slew of new periodicals, though only a few, such as the *Manila Chronicle,* would survive. Joaquin Roces took over where his father Alejandro Sr. left off and revived the *Times,* seeing it climb to a circulation of a quarter million.[6] At the same time, the new channels for communication were beginning to have an effect, most notably radio and television, as both began to move past birth pangs and pains.

Post-war print journalism saw a boom right before the 1972 declaration of martial law by strongman Ferdinand Marcos. Twenty-one dailies, and 100 plus community newspapers were firmly in private hands, and played an increasingly important role as true government watchdog. This was also the time when newspapers cemented one of its more unique qualities: being Manila-centric. Of the 21 dailies, 17 were based in the capital, and of these 9 were in English, elements that continue to pervade Philippine print media today. In any case, the newspapers were buoyed by genuine press freedom even as Marcos watched it warily. Corruption was already somewhat evident then and there was growing concern about newspapers serving as mouthpieces for the big business which owned them. Maslog pointed out how pre-Martial Law media was its best critic.[7] Even then, newspapers began to flex their muscles as catalysts for society, led by more progressive scribes. Arrests were made, and as journalism professor Luis Teodoro points out in *Kasaysayan,* Proclamation 1081 effectively quashed the progressive use of press freedom for actual change.[8]

Sheila Coronel gives a gripping account of that time in *Kasaysayan.* The ominously-titled *Letter of Instruction No. 1* held an ominous effect in itself: It ordered government to take over the various newspapers and broadcast stations and these would be kept under such control for 14 years. All information was screened, and many newspapermen were in jail. Some newspapers would eventually rise from the grave, but firmly in Marcos shackles or in the hands of Marcos friends. *The Daily Express,* the *Times Journal* and the *Manila Bulletin* began peddling the Marcos line as every paper had a military critic looking over all copy. The message was clear: Marcos was watching. Marcos made a show of lifting Martial Law in 1981 and calling elections. But the controls were still in place. And journalists were still being jailed, as evidenced by the almost wholesale arrest of the staff of the critical *We Forum.* It was the assassination of former Senator Benigno "Ninoy" Aquino at the tarmac of the Manila International Airport in 1983 that loosed the hounds. As Malacañang clamped down on reportage of the unrest that was sweeping the country, a new generation of newspapers—the "mosquito press" it was derogatorily called by government—was born.[9]

Letty Jimenez-Magsanoc was a former editor of the *Philippine Panorama* magazine and played a crucial role in that new time, the time for the alternative press. She is editor-in-chief of the *Inquirer.* "It was a curious case of role reversal. The Philippine media did not do its job; the Filipino people did it for them," she wrote in *Kasaysayan.* The brave *Mr. & Ms.* magazine, published by Eugenia Apostol, eventually published a supplement devoted to political news. The *Philippine Inquirer,* also put up by Apostol, began as a chronicle of the Aquino trial. It would eventually go daily and actively took a position that defined news against the mainstream. And it survived on circulation alone, something unheard of until then.[10] The resurgent *Manila Times* and the newly-born *Malaya* were part of this movement, and the 1986 EDSA Revolution galvanized a generation that these new newspapers had nourished with valuable real information. The newspapers' history of feast or famine would again continue.

With Marcos' *Bagong Lipunan* (New Society) over, newspapers experienced another growth spurt as a nation starved for real news lapped it up. Among the new dailies were the *Philippine Star* and the *Manila Standard*. President Corazon Aquino often said that true press freedom was a major part of the legacy she left behind. Unfortunately, the sudden upswing in print and broadcast journalism was also accompanied by the continued deaths of journalists, rising from 2.3 annually during Martial Law to 6 in the Aquino years.[11] Despite that, the press did regain its teeth as it regained the watchdog role it had before Martial Law, a fact that Aquino constantly grappled with. This struggle would culminate in the landmark libel case Aquino won against the *Star*, and specifically, the late respected columnist Luis D. Beltran, a conviction that would later be overturned. These were times of change and quiet turbulence and the press echoed this as well.

The administration under former general Fidel V. Ramos inherited this active press, and Ramos would often find himself both darling and goat to newspapers. One significant development in those years was the organization of the Philippine Center for Investigative Journalism, founded by former *Panorama* and *Chronicle* writer Sheila Coronel, dedicated to independent, in-depth journalism. The PCIJ found itself in the spotlight soon enough after a three-part series they wrote on the President's alleged dalliances with socialite Rosemarie Arenas drew a barrage of criticism. The only paper which ran that series, the *Inquirer*, was immediately embroiled in an ownership tussle that landed it in receivership. While Ramos obviously took efforts to befriend the media, he suffered much criticism as well for such ideas as the national ID system and the charter change. "FVR is not the first president—and he will not be the last—to be unhappy about the press," Adrian Cristobal wrote, ". . . the essential thing to remember is that the freedom and independence—as well as the responsibility of the press is inversely proportionate to the comfort of public officials."[12] This administration also saw the folding of the only newspaper in Tagalog, the *Diario Pilipino*. Another unique newspaper concept that was revived but also proved to be short-lived was the afternoon daily *Evening Paper*.

One interesting development that continued all this time was the uneven performance of the so-called community newspapers. Journalism did not flourish at the grass-roots level, but several papers did endure, greatly dependent on the personalities running them, most notably the hugely successful *Sun-Star Daily* of the south, and the *Punch* of the north. "These community newspapers will rise or fall following the ebbs and tides of the men behind them."[13]

It was during Ramos' term that great optimism surrounding the President's "Philippines 2000" economic program went side-by-side in the news pages with initial signs of brewing economic troubles in Asia. The May 1998 elections proved to be one of the most colorful and the most covered polls in history, and out of that emerged Estrada, a president who exemplified the media-crazy age he now steps into.

Present Tense

The sudden economic crunch that struck Asia badly did not leave newspapers unscathed. Prices of newsprint went up and kept going up, leading newspapers to raise their prices. *The Inquirer*, for example, jumped from P7 to P12 in over a year. But in many ways what was true in the early 1990s was still true in the late '90s, only worse.

With a total of about 30 dailies all in all, the Philippines hosts a majority of tabloids. As of late 1998, there were nine major national dailies: the *Bulletin*, the *Inquirer*, the *Star*, the *Standard*, *Malaya*, *Today*, *Business Daily* and *Business World*, following the folding of the *Chronicle* after a prolonged strike. The ninth daily was a unique broadsheet called *Isyu*, which is almost all opinion, but *Isyu* folded in 1993 due to financial problems.

The market was indeed getting tighter even before the Estrada administration. As early as 1990, a Social Weather Station survey showed that of 1,200 Metro Manila respondents, 49 percent cited television as their primary source of news, while only 24 percent said it was from newspapers, behind even radio's 27 percent.[14] And this was including the numerous tabloids, which were often in Filipino and carried lurid stories and photographs of scantily clad women. And this in a country with one of the best literacy rates in Asia.[15]

Yet all this is indeed part of the riot of ink and inklings that make up the Philippine newspaper scene. The newspapers stagger on, some healthy and growing while others seem to constantly be involved in rumors of dissolution. And they slug it out with government and police over what goes into print, while dealing with the corruption and dangers that come with the job. Then as now.

All the major national dailies are still based in Metro Manila, relying on correspondents in the provinces to keep them up to date. As their editorial and production units are all here, the broadsheets are composed and printed in Manila and are shipped via plane to the provinces and by truck to the city. The broadsheets are sold by both newsstand and subscribers, while the healthy *Business World* is sold exclusively by subscription. Healthy or not, these newspapers all developed unique and distinctive personalities. The tabloids, which gobble up much more in revenues than their broadsheet counterparts, make their lucrative living all from the newsstands.

The shifting of ownership of these dailies is often front-page fodder in itself. It was shortly after the late Betty Go-Belmonte left the *Inquirer* to form the *Star* that boardroom battles began to be waged. It would not be the last ownership struggle over a major newspaper to be covered by their fellow newspapers. The *Inquirer* would eventually be firmly acquired by the Prieto family. The *Inquirer,* just like magnate Emilio Yap's *Manila Bulletin* (Yap followed Hans Menzi as owner) and the *Star* continued to grow. Not even businessman Robert Coyiuto's purchase of the *Chronicle* could ease the bleeding, and a prolonged strike early in 1998 spelled doom for the proud paper. The year 1999 saw two new Filipino breadsheets, *Kababayan* and *Diario Uno*, launched. Two more English breadsheets joined the fray in the form of the *Philippine Post* and the *Sun Star Manila*, a national version of the succesful regional newspaper. But two long-time newspapers folded this year. After being sold by the Gokongweis to a real estate magnate, the *Manila Times*, historic first English daily of Manila, ended its run on July 23. Also writing in 1999 was the government-owned *Times Journal,* the financially-challenged broadsheet of the journal group of companies.

The feud between Estrada and the *Inquirer* continued in 1999. Along with the President's call for amendments to the 1987 constitution, press freedom became a rallying cry for watchdog organizations and activist groups amid Estrada's continued assurances that press freedom was alive and well in the country. All of the events of 1999 only serve as another reminder of the colorful and checkered life story of the Philippines' newspapers at the dawn of the next millenium.

Concern over business interests overtaking the journalistic duty of newspapers remained, but were relatively quiet. It is always and will always be an uneasy marriage, but a necessary one nonetheless. A particular case would be the copy war between the Coyiuto-owned

Chronicle and the Yuchengco-owned *Standard* over the respective businessmen's rivalry in buying the headquarters of Benguet Mining Co. [16] But save for these rare cases like this one, ownership rarely ever enters the editorial realm.

As for the content of newspapers themselves, there would be two clear distinctions, well pointed out by Maslog in *The Metro Manila Press:*

> *One face is that of the broadsheet. The nine broadsheets now publishing are all in English and cater to the political and economic elite and educated middle class. This segment of Philippine society is largely modern and westernized. So are the newspapers which serve them . . .*
>
> *The other face is that of the tabloid. The 20 tabloid newspapers now existing are mostly in Filipino, based largely on Tagalog. They cater to the lower classes . . . They contain mostly human interest stories—sex, crime, oddities . . . even superstition.* [17]

But the lucrative trade that is the tabloids has led to the proliferation of smut, and after years of negligence by the authorities, even the president is getting in on the act. President Estrada recently ordered police to crack down on smut and specified the tabloids, calling for better material for readers. [18]

Because while the numbers are greater, the issues and challenges remain ever the same. The Filipino print journalist remains relatively underpaid and in relative danger. Which is why one of the biggest issues that continues to plague journalists is corruption, especially in a country where it is commonplace. It is not a simple issue. Scandals regarding bribe money up to the National Press Club itself and in press conferences seem to happen time and again. [19] Bribes are explicitly forbidden by the Philippine Journalist's Code of Ethics, but

monitoring is difficult and adherence is voluntary at best. Luz
Rimban hits it on the head when she notes that corruption is a two-
way street between politician and press person. [20] While it would be so
easy to lump the practice of bribe money at every level to the Filipino
concept of *utang na loob* or reciprocated gratitude, it also tends to
leave the corrupt journalist free of blame. It is not merely a matter of
dollars and cents, but of professionalism, yet another problem that
plagues an industry with a high turnover rate and jobs not considered
desirable by fresh graduates.

Future Tense

In a great way, that is the challenge that Luis Teodoro, Dean of the
University of the Philippines College of Mass Communication, cradle
of many a journalist, wrote about in *Kasaysayan*: "Competition has
made newspapers and magazines use almost every means to attract
readership, to the detriment of accuracy, balance and fairness." [21]
Vergel Santos points out that the explosion in media has "depleted the
supply of suitable practitioners and opened the profession to invasion
by pseudo-journalists, resulting in widespread malpractice." [22] It is a
challenge to the media establishment and the media academies to
train new practitioners and steel them against the inevitable tempta-
tions in the real world. It also falls upon watchdog groups such as the
education-oriented Philippine Press Institute and the monitoring
apparatus of the Center for Media Freedom and Responsibility, which
is directed by Melinda Quintos de Jesus and publishes the *Philippine
Journalism Review,* to continue to note and write on correct and incor-
rect practices. It is a rather lonely quest.

For ultimately, it falls upon the newspapers themselves and the
individual reporters to maintain their credibility even when it is

common and practical practice not to have it. New challenges are coming and the newsrooms have changed to face them. Almost all the Metro Manila newspapers are firmly wired, with the electric newsroom now a reality. Martial Law's crackdown was possible because there were no other means of communication aside from those controlled by the government. The microprocessor changed all that, giving birth to the modem, the fax machine and desktop publishing.

Perhaps the newest frontier for newspapers is cyberspace. Most of the dailies are on the Internet and reach out to an international audience immediately. But it apparently is a complement to the real newspapers and not a challenger, at least not in the Philippine setting, where the vast majority of the populace has never owned a computer. The obstacles are three-fold, writes Earl Warren Castillo: the needed information technology "infrastructure" is not in place, Internet access is expensive, and the articles are shortened versions rather than expanded editions of those which appear in the hard copy. Until the computer itself becomes more accessible to Filipinos, "the Internet will remain a non-competitor of the print medium." [23]

In other words, newspapers are safe for now. But are we safe from them? As the newspapers move closer to the new millenium and past the first Centennial, the very same issues continue to be discussed, continue to be relevant, from the youngest reader to well, the most important one.

This was probably foremost in Estrada's mind when he met with the presidential press corps on July 18, 1998. "I'm too new as your president so I do appeal to you to give me a chance." [24] It was a delicious, comedic twist: The most powerful man in the land, at the most crucial time in history, asking the press to give him a chance, to go easy on him. Indeed, Estrada knows a thing or two about newspapers and the like, including one undeniable truth: For good or ill, they are both going to be here a while.

NOTES

1. *Philippine Daily Inquirer,* 16 July 1998.

2. *Inquirer,* 14 August 1998.

3. Maria Aurora Gelvezon and Pamela Stephanie Muñoz "Elections '98 Coverage," *Philippine Journalism Review,* April-June 1998, pp.14-21.

4. Crispin C. Maslog, The Metro Manila Press, (Manila: Philippine Press Institute, 1994), pp. 1-5.

5. Ibid., pp. 6-8.

6. Ibid., pp. 17-24.

7. Ibid., pp. 25-32.

8. Luis V. Teodoro, "Postwar Philippine Journalism," *Kasaysayan: The Story of the Filipino People,* vol. 8 (Manila: Asia Publishing Co., Ltd.), pp. 94-95.

9. Sheila S. Coronel, "The Marcos Media," *Kasaysayan: The Story of the Filipino People,* vol. 9 (Manila: Asia Publishing Co., Ltd.), pp. 154-155.

10. Letty Jimenez-Magsanoc, "The Alternative Press," *Kasaysayan: The Story of the Filipino People,* vol. 9 (Manila: Asia Publishing Co., Ltd.), pp. 264-265.

11. Ed Aurelio C. Reyes, *Press Freedom: The People's Right* (Manila: Phil. Movement for Press Freedom, 1992), pp. 132-133.

12. *Inquirer,* 28 September 1992.

13. Crispin C. Maslog, *The Rise and Fall of Community Newspapers* (Manila: Philippine Press Institute, 1993), pp. 1-32.

14. Red Batario, "Market Squeeze," *Philippine Journalism Review,* August 1990, pp. 15-16.

15. Ronald P. Jacinto, "Re-engineering the Educational System," MBC Business Papers, July 1994, pp. 9-12.

16. Ian Neri, "Newspapers as a Tool of Business Interests," *Philippine Journalism Review,* 1993, p. 11.

17. Maslog, *Manila Press,* p. 53.

18. *Inquirer,* 11 September 1998.

19. Melinda Quintos de Jesus, *Philippine Journalism Review,* December 1991, pp. 20-21.

20. Luz Del Rosario-Rimban, "Corruption, a Two-way Street Between Politicians and the Press," *Philippine Journalism Review,* December 1991, pp. 33-34.

21. Teodoro, *Kasaysayan,* p. 95.

22. Vergel Santos, "Philippine Media in Transition," *Philippine Journalism Review,* April 1990, p. 31.

23. Earl Warren D. Castillo, "Responding To The Digital Challenge," *Philippine Journalism Review,* December 1997, pp. 27-30.

24. *Inquirer,* 19 July 1998.

FINDING YOUR VOICE: THE BILINGUAL WRITER'S DILEMMA

Paulino Lim, Jr.

The literary term "voice" is often used interchangeably with style but, whereas style can be accurately described, voice can only be approximated. Style can be shown to be colloquial or literary, latinate or Anglo-Saxon, terse or long-winded, by looking at the writer's diction, tropes and sentence structures. These elements can also be used to interpret voice but may not be sufficient, especially in such contexts as Blake's songs of innocence and experience when voice becomes synonymous with point of view, or a description of voice as prophetic that appropriates both tone and theme.

Given the links of voice with artistic autonomy and the fluid linguistic medium which too often eludes the author's control—expecially when it yields deconstructive meanings—one sees the difficulty of trying to define a writer's voice, much less trying to look for one. The issue becomes more complicated when applied to bilingual writers in the Philippines, including those who have migrated to English-speaking countries such as Australia, England and the United States, who are capable of writing both in English and in another native language. This essay addresses the question of voice as part of a larger dilemma that a Filipino writer in English faces. This can be baldly stated thus: To write in English in the U.K. or the U.S. is to adopt the language of the dominant culture; to write English in the Philippines is to perpetuate a colonized culture. Not fully conversant with the adopted culture, the immigrant writer risks being marginalized or, worse, rendered mute. Whereas in the Philippines English marginalizes the writer in another sense as being elitist, out of touch with the masses; furthermore, it prevents the writer from participating in the development of a "true" Philippine literature. This essay sketches the history behind this dilemma and relates voice to questions about self and sensibility. For example, does the writer have an essential self that is revealed in his or her work? Does the writing exhibit a sensibility, a way of thinking or feeling that is characteristic of a country, its time and place in history?

The bilingual capability of the Filipino writer is acknowledged by the Philippine Centennial Commission which sponsored in 1998 a literary contest "about the ideas and events of the Philippine Revolution of 1896 and their aftermath." There were five categories: epic poetry, novel, drama, essay and screenplay. Filipino and English were the languages for the competition, with Spanish allowed for the epic poetry category. The Spanish entry, *Mujer Indegena* by Carmelo Nadera, won second prize. The first prize for each category was a decisive million pesos. Winners, such as Cirilo Bautista for his epic poem *Sunlight on Broken Stones* and Eric Gamalinda for his novel *My Sad Republic,* became known as "literary millionaires."

A Filipino writer can write in his first language, such as Hiligaynon or Bicol, and also in Filipino—the national language he learns at school. He may even write in Chinese or Spanish, if the family spoke the language or sent him to special schools to study it. Chances are he practised his craft by writing in English, which he has studied since grade school. He also dreams of having a wider readership in English for either journalism or literature than in his first or second language.

A Visayan writer may draft a manifesto in Cebuano to complain about the fact that Tagalog was chosen as the basis for the country's national language which, incidentally, had a name change from Pilipino to Filipino in the post-dictatorship 1987 Constitution. Likewise, in one of the many ongoing language debates, the Tagalog professor of English may write in Filipino to underscore the colonized mentality of native authors who choose English, which they do not speak at home. The regional Visayan or nationalist Tagalog must know somehow that it's all gesture, seeing that in Cebu the Tagalog periodicals outsell the Visayan and in Manila bookstores more than 90% of the volumes on display are in English. (Azurin 1993: 194)

This is not to suggest that the country's literature in English is the most dominant. But for an Iluko or Tagalog poem to be widely read, it better be translated into two other languages, English being one them. Such was the case of the 1988-89 recipients of writing grants awarded by the Cultural Center of the Philippines. The writers—Benjamin M. Pascual, Leo Bob Flores, and Lina Sagaral Reyes—wrote in Iluko, Cebuano and English, respectively. Their poems were published in an anthology with Filipino and English translations. [*Handurawan* 1990] The anthology recognizes that a Muslim reader from Mindanao who may not comprehend either the Iluko or Cebuano text can surely read either or both Filipino and English. In a land of many tongues English is a language not only of meditation but also of mediation.

Invoking the image of "the wounded diamond," Leonard Casper, the foremost American critic of Philippine literature in English, sees the creative writer as a cutter who has to cut a diamond along its flaws. The flaws that shape the Filipino's telling, according to Casper, are society's dilemmas, its language difficulties, and his own personal mysteries. (1964: 5) This suggests that the art itself may be flawed or that the artist is hurting. One can take this lapidary metaphor to launch either into a cool analysis of the past or a hot critique of the present. F. Sionil Jose, whose Philippine novels are being published by Random House, implicates both undertaking when he writes: "We may have survived 300 years of Spanish tyranny, forty years of grudging American benevolence and three brutal years of Japanese occupation but we continue to languish in the prison created by this past." (1988: 45)

Earnest scrutiny of the country's past and present may throw light on the flaws of the diamond, or throw one into a fault-finding rut. Surely, colonialism can be faulted for compelling dependency and nurturing inferiority. The Spanish and American colonizers preached that theirs was the superior culture, theirs the superior race. At a time when Cultural Studies has become an academic discipline, along with Deconstruction and New Historicism, the Spaniards are being faulted for their role in eradicating valuable information about the country's precolonial culture written in the native syllabary. In the words of critic and literary historian Bienvenido Lumbera, "the perishable materials on which the Filipinos wrote were left to disintegrate and those that remained were destroyed by missionaries who believed the indigenous pagan culture was the handicraft of the devil himself." (1982: 3) Many also fault the Americans for not allowing Spanish to develop alongside the English or Anglo-Saxon tradition. It was a matter of expediency for the essentially monolingual American colonizers, whose own founding fathers had to vote on whether to adopt English or German. Indeed, one language has the capacity to unite a people, two the potential to divide, as in the case of Canada, where the French-speaking region wants to secede from the English majority.

The fact remains, however, that when the would-be Filipino writers in English were starting to learn the literary medium from the American colonizers during the first two decades of the 1900's, the literature written in Spanish by their forebears was reaching its "golden age." According to Pilar Marino, who has compiled and translated a fiction anthology of the literature, poetry was the most important achievement of this golden age but it was "the short story in Spanish which inspired the most and best writers." The writers drew sympathetic characters from the middle and low classes and produced narratives that "strongly resemble the short stories of the French writers Alphonse Daudet, Guy de Maupassant, and Prosper Merimee." The stories ranged in types from beast fables to fairy tales, in techniques from the character sketch to the epistolary, and in tones from tragic to satiric. In spite of their differences, they were linked by two characteristics: concern with ethical issues and mastery of the Spanish language. Professor Marino considers the Filipino short story in Spanish as "one of the most precious legacies of Philippine colonial literature." (1989: xxv)

It is important to note that recovery of this colonial legacy, including the subversive Spanish novels of Jose Rizal—who was executed by the Spaniards and made national hero by the Filipinos—requires its translation into English. The language was a casualty of the nationalistic resurgence of the late 1960s; until then 12 units of Spanish was mandatory for college graduation. (A similar campaign to do away with English as the medium of instruction started soon after; professors at the University of the Philippines and other colleges, who have the option to choose either Filipino or English, usually end up using both.) The task of recovery is similar to what is being done with pre-colonial and ethnic literatures. Filipino scholars, however, report that translating from one Philippine language, such as from Bicol to Tagalog or Filipino, poses no problem; both have the same syntax and, although the terms differ, "there is practically a one-to-one correspondence of lexical items." (Erestain 1994-95: 83) The problem comes with the English translation, especially when no English word corresponds to the original, or when a native metaphor or idiom makes no sense in any foreign translation.

This linguistic problem highlighting the disparity between the syntax and lexicon of English and the Philippine languages is complicated by two other related issues—social and political. English has become the language of the intellectual elite, just as Spanish was before the Americans came. Unlike the Spaniards who did not teach their language to the masses, the Americans made English the medium of instruction in all Philippine schools. The Spanish policy kept the country divided but also alienated the people from the colonial administration; the American policy pacified a recalcitrant population that initially fought a war similar to the one waged by the Vietnamese. Whatever the result, antipathy towards Spain and sympathy for the U.S., both languages are regarded as instruments of colonialism or neo-colonialism. The latter relates to the perception that, although the U.S. granted the Philippines independence in 1946, it has kept its hold on the country's affairs. The U.S. support of the dictatorship of Marcos against the communist insurgency and of Corazon Aquino against a rebellious military strengthened this belief.

In the 1970s the bilingual Filipino writer choosing for artistic expression between his native language and English had to consider not just ease or mastery of either medium. He knew that the former enabled him to speak to the masses, the latter aligned him with the intellectual and political elite, which the insurgency wanted to overthrow. The communist victory in Vietnam signalled the possibility that the repressive Marcos dictatorship would also fall. For the writer the choice between Filipino and English seemed like a decision between loving and betraying one's country. According to renowned critic Epifanio San Juan, who sees an insidious intent as well as effect of America's educational policy, "English (administered through public education) became for the U.S. the necessary mechanism for the subordination of the Filipino people to the global project of laissez-faire 'free trade' guided by U.S. Finance capital." (1988: 25) He concludes that a half century of English teaching perpetuated serfdom in the countryside and alienated the English-using intellectuals from workers and peasants speaking the vernacular. It is the latter charge that the Filipino writer in English takes to heart the most. He may have "found" a voice in his adopted medium, but is it "true" to his subject, his experience as a Filipino. He is aware of the belief that the various vernaculars share the same complexity of meanings that perhaps best express the Filipino psyche, long misread by psychologists using Western tools of analysis and inadequate translations of the native languages.

It was not always the case before this period of heightened nationalist consciousness. Before then, the test was whether the writers were true to the experience using an adopted medium of expression. In other words, the writers had to respond to the charge whether the English medium remained true to the experience and sensibilty of the Philippine subject. Thus, a writer like Manuel Arguilla, who published before the Second World War, was praised for his "attempt to coalesce and synthesize indigenous materials and foreign form through the English language to create a structural unity distinctly Filipino in values and qualities." (Hosillos 1969: 79) Structural unity was a key idea at the time of this assessment, when Formalism or New Criticism defined the norms for the artistic merit of literary works and dominated critical discourse. Later, of course, the criterion of structural unity collapsed when newer techniques of analysis were brought into play, shifting emphasis for example from a psychology grounded in biology (Freud) to one based in language (Lacan). This has resulted in questioning essentialist theories, such as whether an author has a "self" to express, or that his work exhibits the country's "sensibility," which is definable in any medium of expression and quite distinct from it.

The remark by Nick Joaquin, considered the greatest Filipino writer in English, about the young writers in the early 1960s is interesting: "These young boys today—they are making it their English. It may not be the English of America, or the English of the English. It's some sort of terrifying English." (1964: 81-82) "Terrifying" could very well describe some of Joaquin's prose, although in the climactic scene of his well-known short story, "The Summer Solstice," the feeling might be induced by something else:

She raised her skirts and contemptuously thrust out a naked foot. He lifted his dripping face and touched his bruised lips to her toes; lifted his hands and grasped the white foot and kissed it savagely—kissed the step, the sole, the frail ankle—while she bit her lips and clutched in pain at the windowsill her body distended and wracked by horrible shivers, her head flung back and her loose hair streaming out the window—streaming fluid and black in the white night where the huge moon glowed like a sun and the dry air flamed into lightning and the pure heat burned with the immense intense fever of noon. (1982: 325)

About the same time that Gabriel Garcia Marquez was writing "magic realism," Filipino writer Wilfredo D. Nolledo was writing the same kind of prose—in English. The English translation of Marquez's *One Hundred Years of Solitude* and Nolledo's *But for the Lovers* were both published in 1970. The latter was reissued in 1996, a testimony to its durability as literature. Here is the opening of Nolledo's *Canticle for Dark Lovers* which was published in *Short Story International* in 1964:

It had been a night for lovers and today the morning was sunlight in the face and in the city held by building and man both, the birds flew out of the trees and met together in the east where they flew for their food. Under them, cats of the night tumbled over garbage cans and prowled the world left by pedestrians. It had also been a night for scavengers and they collided at the mouths of debris, scratching the cats away, hauling back broken conditions to be made new again, scraps, demented favors, the bottoms of bottles where still hung back the sweetness of milk or the tang of wine. Snarling and snatching, the beggars multiplied and very soon the dogs came, too. (21)

How does one relate Joaquin's fervid prose and Nolledo's lyricism to something which may be called Filipino sensibility? Does the sensibility remain constant whether expressed by a feminist or a Chinese Filipino like Charlson Ong, whose English novel *Embarrassment of Riches* won second prize in the Centennial Literary Contest. Perhaps, magic realism or tropical baroque is a much more demonstrable attribute, starting with a comparison of texts that literary criticism identifies as examples of the genre, and analysis of their syntax. Still, to writer/critic Isagani R. Cruz, who writes both Filipino and English criticisms, there is such a thing as a Filipino sensibility. Cruz has also strenuously argued that Filipino English is not English and that the latter "has too limited a vocabulary for dealing with Philippine social realities." (1996: 130)

As the country's most influential critic, Cruz has drawn a hypothetical map of Philippine writing in the late 1980s, identifying the "four points on the compass [as] gender, class, race, and language." (1996: 155) The compass point of gender directs one to feminist and gay literature and criticism. Class can refer broadly to the struggle between the poor majority and rich minority, or narrowly to the "prostitution of the Filipino intellectual elite." Cruz illustrates how "the white, Anglo-Saxon race, monolithic in impact . . . impinges without mercy even on the most hospitable English text written by Filipinos." For the fourth category, Cruz distinguishes between Philippine and American English, as well as the language of postcolonial societies. (1996:155)

The nationalistic intransigence toward English has softened against the realities of the global economy. American cartoon producers, who have their television cartoons drawn by artists in Asia in search of cheap labor, prefer the Philippines because "Filipinos have a Western sense of humor. . . . They speak English. They know America." (Drogin 1993) The ability to speak the language, even if it does not come across like the Queen's English, enables Filipinos to work aboard a Norwegian cruise ship, an oil rig in Saudi Arabia, and a hospital in California. The country is grateful for the dollars these overseas workers send to their families, regular remittances that tremendously help the economy. This economic reality may have prompted educators to mandate 80 minutes of each school day in the elementary schools for English instruction. Does this policy of education signal that English will continue as a second language in the Philippines and not become a "foreign" language? This is apparently the case in Hong Kong since its return to China in 1997. Will future Filipino writers have to answer the charge that their voice in English is not authentic, not indicative of their true self, and invariably reflects a colonized sensibility?

A defense may be marshalled against the claim, made by Cruz and others, that English is inadequate to deal with Philippine social realities because of its limited vocabulary. Eskimos have made a similar claim concerning the inadequacy of the English translation for their experience of "snow" for which they have an abundant vocabulary. Filipino easily converts nouns into abstractions, for example, *bata* and *kabataan* for "child" and "childhood." In contrast, speakers of English would hesitate to use "seahood" or "oceanness" in the same context as *karagatan*, the abstract noun for *dagat*. As a result Filipino produces richer meanings for sea and ocean, only hinted at in such phrases as "all at sea," and "sea change." By the same token, Filipino would have to do verbal gymnastics to convey the meaning of the marvelous English phrase "sea legs."

Strange as it may seem, words alone do not convey the reality or truth writers aim to express or readers perceive in the work. To borrow an analogy from Heidegger, words are like the stones that Grecian masons use to build a temple on a craggy Aegean hillside. (1977: 168) The words in the literary work cease to be mere tools of expression, just as the stones cease to be more than mere building blocks. The finished work speaks a distinctive voice, and whether this voice is sensual or reverential depends upon whether the temple honors Venus as the goddess of love or Apollo the god of poetry. This voice radiates from the work like film images projected on the screen of the reader's consciousness. Voice is what readers "hear," and what they hear is not always what is being said. To describe this voice by analyzing style may produce the equivalent of a voiceprint, a visual record of speech with respect to frequency, duration, and amplitude. But it won't suffice; one has to describe tone and write words similar to what one reads on wine labels.

Perhaps, writers should not worry about finding a voice or expressing an authentic self and sensibility as much as producing the best that they are capable of doing with whatever language they choose. Despite what Cruz says about the limitations of the Filipino writers in English, publishing in New Manila, New York or New Zealand, they can take heart from what he has concluded about their work, that it "has to be one of the most vibrant and rich literatures being written in English anywhere in the world today."

REFERENCES

Azurin, Arnold Molina. 1993. *Reinventing the Filipino: Sense of Being and Becoming.* Diliman, Quezon City: University of the Philippines Press.

Casper, Leonard. 1964. *The Wounded Diamond.* Manila: Bookmark.

Cruz, Isagani R. 1996. *The Alfred E. Litiaco Lectures of Isagani Cruz.* Ed. David Jonathan Bayot. Manila: De La Salle University Press.

Drogin, Bob. 1993. Cartoon Stars Take Around-the-World Cruise. *Los Angeles Times,* 30 March: H6.

Erestain, Teresita F. 1994-95. A Poem in Three Voices: An Exercise in Translation. *Likha 15: 73-85.*

Handurawan: Antolohiya ng mga Tula ng mga Tumanggap ng CCP Literature Grants 1988-1989. 1990. Manila: Cultural Center of the Philippines.

Heidegger, Martin. 1977. *Basic Writings*. Ed. David Farrell Krell. New York, Harper and Row.

Hosillos, Lucila V. 1969. *Philippine-American Literary Relations*. Diliman, Quezon City: University of the Philippines Press.

Joaquin, Nick. 1982. The Summer Solstice. In Bienvenido Lumbera, ed., *Philippine Literature*. Manila: National Book Store.

_____. 1964. "The Young Writers." In *Literature and Society: A Symposium on the Relation of Literature to Social Change*. Manila: Alberto S. Florentino.

Jose, F. Sionil. 1988. "Art, Life and the Filipino Soul." In Edwin Thumboo, ed., *Literature and Liberation*. Manila: Solidaridad Publishing House.

Lumbera, Bienvenido, and Cynthia N. Lumbera. 1982. *Philippine Literature: A History and Anthology*. Manila: National Book Store.

Marino, Pilar E., comp., ed. and trans. 1989. *Philippine Short Stories in Spanish 1900-1941*. Diliman, Quezon City: University of the Philippines Office of Research Coordination.

Nolledo, Wilfredo D. 1964. Canticle for Dark Lovers. *Short Story International*. August: 21-36.

San Juan, E. Jr. 1988. *Ruptures, Schisms, Interventions: Cultural Revolution in the Third World*. Manila: De La Salle University Press.

WRITING FAST, WRITING QUICKLY— HEAR YOUR VOICE AND DROP THAT STEREOTYPE

Nadine Sarreal

A couple of years ago, in a casual conversation with a prominent and well-respected writer in the Philippines, I introduced myself as a Filipino-American writer. He told me impatiently that one is either a Filipino writer or an American writer, that there is no such thing as a Filipino-American. Perhaps he was irritated with *balikbayan* writers who published both in the United States and in the Philippines, thus sucking away meager publishing resources from local writers. From his facial expression, I could see he had dismissed me and I kept my arguments to myself, being Filipina enough to respect my elders even when I think they are wrong.

There *is* such a thing as a Filipino-Amerian writer. I know because that is what I am. I contain the simultaneously conflicting and supportive sensibilities of an American and a Filipina. However, my early fiction didn't address my personal schism. Reading my work from the 1970s and 80s, I see that my characters were unrooted, free floating people, usually concerned with some small yet universal matters, perhaps money for groceries. It wasn't until Cecilia Brainard introduced me to the concept of voice that I faced my internal dichotomy squarely. I'm not here to tell you that I've found a way to meld my eastern and western minds, because I haven't. What I want to say is that, in my experience, anyone who straddles two cultures will always write from a place of discomfort and unease.

I believe that as Filipino-American writers, we aren't just trying to create fiction but are also synthesizing our identities from which to pour stories.

There is a comforting balance in that our work can be based on two cultures. We can draw from both. It's like having two palettes with very different hues and tones at our fingertips as we paint word pictures.

And why should we not know both *Kano* and *Pinoy* minds? Our lives have somehow gone back and forth between the two countries. Perhaps we are Filipino-American because one parent was white and the other brown. Or we came to this sub-minority because we were born here, and grew up there, or vice versa, or were shuttled back and forth during our formative years, having to learn and unlearn English, Tagalog, Ilocano or Hiligaynon, depending on where we were and who we had to speak with. Our various histories and backgrounds made us a mixed breed, if not genetically, then experientially. In America, we are not white. In the Philippines, we are *balikbayan*, treated differently, too. So where is home for us?

In our hearts, we think of ourselves as transnationals with deep allegiances and a critical sense of identification with two cultures and countries. While *El Niño* pours a deluge of precipitation on America, we also worry about the counterpart drought in the Philippines.

Often, though, a person who tries to bridge two cultures ends up alienating both sides. There is no pleasing anyone. There is no real belonging. Often, we face stereotypes, both here and in the Philippines. Thanks to Hollywood and television, Asians are often characterized as sinister villains and dragon ladies in martial arts movies. Or comical servants and loyal sidekicks like Kato to the Pink Panther. Despite the anthology, *Charlie Chan is dead,* Asian men with eyeglasses are still lumped together as ascetic, asexual geeks. It's easy to accept stereotypes. John Streamas, in his article "The Search for Writing Becomes Discovery of Self," identifies three main persisting stereotypes of the Asian:

1) the model minority student, humorless and hard-working, who turns into a nerdy scientist or mathematician

2) the boat person refugee from a war-ravaged nation, poor, shy, ill-educated, grateful for American hospitality while at the same time, fearful of perceived xenophobia

3) the media-packaged emasculated or kung-fu fighting men and their exotic, sexually submissive women.

On the other hand, the stereotype of the American in the Filipino mind embodies the characteristics of being friendly, direct (sometimes to the point of tactlessness), clumsy, wealthy, wasteful, shallow and sexually fixated. Americans don't raise their children properly and don't treat their elders with respect. Americans value efficiency, without regard for human relationships or a higher being that binds them with the rest of humanity.

Within the Filipino culture, we attribute certain types of behavior to people from the various regions of the country. Ilocanos are hard-working and tight-fisted; Tagalogs, easy-going and lazy; Visayans, sweet-natured but simple-minded. Kapampangans are great cooks but treacherous in tough times. We've heard the jokes about the different dialects and sub-cultures and we've laughed at them, too. These stereotypes allow a common basis for our laughter.

Stereotypes have a preliminary sociological function, of course. They give us a view of people different from ourselves, based on our own observations and comments from those whose opinions and attitudes resemble our own. As Filipino-American writers, though, we have to transcend these stereotypes, to allow our own identities to emerge. Identity is crucial to a writer, for we write what we know. And we have to know the difference between stereotyping and characterization.

If we write of things that relate to our particular slice of life and experience, there will be few people able to relate to the stories. The counter-argument is that the human experience is universal and culture is merely a trapping, an external cloak that the fiction describes and then lifts away in order to reveal the story truth that lies beneath. Yet readers have had, to my way of thinking, strange reactions to the cloaks in my stories.

At a recent writing workshop, I presented a story about a Filipina maid working for an American woman in Hong Kong. There was an immediate and strong negative response from one of the group leaders—this is WRONG she said. Why? I asked. She couldn't articulate her reasons adequately but I sensed she prided herself on her democratic and liberal feminist views. I think she meant that a woman of color should not be presented as working for a white woman from a progressive country. She was imposing her political and humanitarian views on my fiction. Perhaps limited perspective is her problem, not mine. I believe she never lifted the cloak and never got on to the next level of my story. And if this same person or someone who holds similar views is an editor or reader at a literary journal or a publishing house, then my work is put aside before it is fully considered.

Part of our identity problem is that externally, the Filipino culture closely resembles western cultures. After 500 years of exposure to occidental thinking and manners, we have adopted many external trappings. A Filipino writer friend contends that Filipinos seem to assimilate so quickly into American like. We do this to survive and get ahead, but the cost is that we lose many opportunities to examine who we are.

Friends and teachers who read my work often comment that the stories are enriched because of the Filipino elements in my fiction. I don't use my work to exploit Filipino culture by high-lighting what American readers perceive as foreign and exotic. I want my stories to be about people who happen to be Filipino.

I want to talk about two simple techniques that have helped me get beyond my own stereotypes and broaden my writing.

The first technique incorporates what Dorothea Brande, in her book, *Becoming a Writer*, calls harnessing the unconscious. She describes it thus:

The best way to do this is to rise half an hour, or a full hour, earlier than you customarily rise. Just as soon as you can—and without talking, without reading the morning's paper, without picking up the book you laid aside the night before—begin to write. Write anything that comes into your head; last night's dream, if you are able to remember it; the activities of the day before; a conversation, real or imaginary; an examination of conscience. Write any sort of early morning reverie, rapidly and uncritically. The excellence or ultimate worth of what you write is of no importance yet. As a matter of fact, you will find more value in this mate-rial than you expect, but your primary purpose now is not to bring forth deathless words.

I would like to emphasize her call to write rapidly and uncritical-ly. Write so quickly that you don't have time to set up a value system in the words that stream from your mind through your pen. Write so fast that your critic's voice doesn't have a chance to establish itself in your head. Trust, instead, that small inner voice that is just waking up with stories long hidden, grievances that need airing, ecstasies that have to be expressed.

After following Ms. Brande's suggestions several times, I altered the procedure to find a method that worked better for me. I'm not an early morning riser to begin with and if I wake up, the rest of the fam-ily wakes up, too, and wants into my consciousness. They want break-fast, they want to talk baseball and work problems, school business. So since I had experienced tapping into my unconscious I knew what the state felt like. Now I had to recreate the same conditions under other circumstances. I experimented over a period of a week and found that for me, sitting comfortably in a public place and relaxing could evoke the same link to my unconscious. Some of the places that work well for me are shopping mall benches, fast food courts, sidewalk cafes, the corner table in the public library, and one of those big, cushy chairs in a Barnes and Noble store. I think these places afford me a special kind of anonymity and privacy and yet also give me a white noise that quiets my critical voice.

The writing I produce in conjunction with my unconscious self does not set out to correct any perceived social wrongs or evils. Without this kind of agenda, my words are truer and have a smaller risk of depending on stereotypes.

This technique of harnessing the unconscious will provide a writer two things—a way to loosen up and sink to a level of freer thinking and feeling, and second, a bunch of words on a lot of paper. I periodically go back over my free writing and mine it for themes or issues (big OR small) that concern my uncritical self. These themes are usually already imbedded in my conscious work, but perhaps wrapped up and disguised. By becoming aware of the themes through my unconscious exercises, I can heighten them in my conscious work. Doing this generally adds new energy to whatever story I am working on. I've also noticed that my unconscious writing is more poetic and lyrical, spilling some of my artist's reservoir on paper, though, then it's mine to use even in the presence of the critical voice.

The second anti-stereotype technique is one I apply during early revision of a story or novel excerpt. As I read my work aloud, even if it's just a rough draft, I look for words that sound judgmental and thus stereotypical. There are places where such words are appropriate, such as when I am writing from a character's point of view or in dialogue. Words like "good," "bad," "humble," "simple," "small," "bony," and "arrogant" can be revealing about a character. However, I want to make sure that I, as the author, am not forcing my feelings about a thing or a person upon the reader with words that don't carry literary value.

To write, "I was born to a poor, humble family" says to the reader that I think I was born to such a family. It is my opinion. And that's fine if my opinion is part of the fiction I'm trying to create. However, if I write, "In my family, we wore our shoes very carefully. After all, we had one pair each and it had to last the whole school year," then hopefully, I've covered poverty and humility and I've also given the reader something tangible with which to enter my fiction.

And importantly, I haven't foisted my character on the reader as someone who was poor and self-righteously humble.

As an author, I try to be aware of what biases I employ in my fiction. Do I portray a woman as the automatically weaker sex? I hope not. Do my Filipino characters have to be inherently naïve and less sophisticated than my western characters? Definitely not. It's a matter of seeing my work with more objective eyes, and not necessarily changing my personal beliefs and attitudes. By replacing or eliminating weak adjectives like "poor" and "simple," I can re-write my story at a different level, so that the characters become free of my opinions. I know this must sound contradictory since my characters are borne from my imagination. However, as a "parent" to these people in my fiction, I want the best for them and want to release them from my personal limitations.

In conclusion, I'd like to encourage Filipino-American writers to write quickly, turning a deaf ear to the critical voice inside you. Keep a journal. Take notes about your dreams. Write all the time. Read as much Filipino and Filipino-American writing as your eyes will allow. We're all in this together, creating ourselves and breaking out of stereotypical thinking.

RADICALIZING THE IMAGE: THE REVOLUTIONARY PHILIPPINE FEMININE IN POETRY

Luisa A. Igloria

While living in Chicago from 1992-1996, working on my Ph.D. and teaching in the university, I became involved with several community-based Filipino American organizations including the cultural and theater group PINTIG (Tagalog for *pulse*). PINTIG had various networks of support, and its energies in organizing and outreach were to a large extent aided by two other activist groups: a broader coalition called the Alliance for Philippine Concerns (APC), and the *Pinay* solidarity network GABRIELA. I quickly became involved with both, and in particular, the women of Gabriela extended an invitation—first to give poetry readings on their behalf, alongside local Chicano, Puerto Rican, Korean American, Chinese American and African American writers and second to join cultural workers in local

239

multicultural programs. Many participants (third or fourth generation) were interested in deepening their knowledge of their literary and cultural heritage.

Eventually I did both, though it was with some hesitation that I initially considered the latter invitation, because any previous "involvements" that I had with the women's movement were more informal in nature. Mostly the connection had come by way of the themes, subjects, contents and my strivings for form. I was engaged by the search for a distinct poetic voice and identity that would allow a freedom to investigate both individual and collective experiences, without feeling constricted by or beholden to conventional poetic strategies.

During the years that I taught with the University of the Philippines in Baguio, I had helped to organize a lecture series on women's issues and had been sent as a delegate to several national and regional workshops on the institution of women's studies at the tertiary level. I was also in touch with women writers who were my friends, colleagues or former teachers, and when some of them proposed the formation of the collective called Women Interested in Creating Cultural Alternatives (WICCA), I registered both my interest and support. But in addition to these, I had never affixed a label either on myself or on my writing that consciously or deliberately bestowed upon them or highlighted their feminist nature; however, reading my poetry before a variety of groups, I found that people were able to identify strongly with the "women's issues," the "feminist concerns," and the "feminist voice" that they found in my work. They also commented on the recurrence, in my poems, of content and imagery that allowed them to read woman's experience concurrent with the experience of moments of patriotic identification and/or nostalgia. In other words, though I was largely unconscious of such an agenda, when I read my work it would sometimes happen that I was no longer myself, an individual poet with an individual and specific biography, reading—but more pointedly a cipher for something larger than myself—perhaps, a Filipino woman reading. Or, if you like, especially during the times that I participated in multicultural women's fora for and on behalf of GABRIELA, both a Filipino woman reading, and a GABRIELA woman reading.

These were issues of identity and representation and they impinged on the individual writing process in interesting ways. They both transfixed and mystified me, and I sought to understand in a deeper way their significance for both myself and my writing practice. In the most basic terms, this was the way I posed the problem to myself: First, in what ways was I meant to consider an indebtedness to the claims of a radical or radicalizing set of images in my personhood and in my poetry? Second, after having established the ways in which certain images informed and shaped the contours of this poetic land-scape, how could I view them in terms of their emergence from and relation to certain traditions or conventions attached to imaging women/the imaging of woman in Philippine literature at large, and in poetry specifically?

Reading poetry on diasporic, migrant and overseas Filipino workers' experiences, and speaking on the history of Filipino women's writing at a Filipino American Women's Network (FAWN)-sponsored conference in St.Paul, Minnesota as a GABRIELA delegate in August 1996 gave me another chance to go over the marks describing the trajectory of women's writing in the Philippines and review it as a history that might have been characterized as writing on or from the fringes, of "invisible" writing prone to erasure and merely accommodative practices—but as one produced by nevertheless always-already-historically-there presences.

Most of the existing sources on women's literary history predictably cite as exemplary the cases of women like Magdalena Jalandoni and Leona Florentino; but many, like Marjorie Evasco and Rosalinda Pinedo Ofreneo, also exhort us to remember that there are other important sources for the images of woman; that there are many voices and threads making up this tradition and that women have practiced other forms of "writing" their experiences, *cuentos* or stories, especially in those cases when the opportunity to leave more conventional forms of inscription (those valued by a text-centered culture) was denied them because the production of literature was related to the enjoyment of certain class privileges.

However that may be, when an analysis is made of the images of woman, of Filipino womanhood recurring in historical fable and in different forms of women's writing, a set of powerful references can be identified. Without necessarily implying that a binary relationship exists between them or that these are the only types of images that exist of Filipino women, I wish to highlight at this point the referential images of *Inang Bayan* or Motherland, and of the heroic-revolutionary Filipina character as typified by the figure of Gabriela Silang (also the original reference for the organization GABRIELA and the embodiment of its nationalist/feminist liberative aims), and examine their iconic and generative usefulness in some samples of contemporary women's narrativizations and poetry.

In this paper neither do I claim to be able to do an exhaustive survey of available literature, in the interest of pursuing these questions. Instead, I draw on a more limited field represented by some of my own poetry, some of the writings or narratives of contemporary Filipino poets, and examples provided by the poetry collected in the volume *Pangarap at Hinagpis: Mga Awit ng Kababaihang Maralita (Dreams and Woes: Songs of Poor Women)* edited by Aida F. Santos and jointly published by GABRIELA and the Institute of Women's Studies in Manila (1991).

Woman as Nation: Suffering Woman

A popular patriotic song, often sung at public rallies, protests and demonstrations as well as during the events surrounding the 1986 People's Power Revolution as an alternative national anthem, images the Motherland or Nation as a woman ravaged by [foreign] oppressors ("*At sa kaniyang yumi at ganda/ Dayuhan ay nahalina/ Bayan ko, binihag ka/ Nasadlak sa dusa...* "). She is an abject figure enchained by her suffering, and the patriotic call sounded by the lyrics is meant to incite her children-citizens to rise not only to her defense but to the procurement of her freedom. She is both the goal of revolutionary acts and fervor, and the traumatized body emblematic of the causes necessitating revolution in the first place.

If, as Benedict Andersen puts it in *Imagined Communities*, the "deep, horizontal comradeship" felt by a citizenry in solidarity with others results from a creative act—the ability to first of all imagine such a model of relation—then the image of country or nation-as-Mother (for whom children, out of their filial loyalty for her, are bent to profess as the ultimate act of love their willingness to give up their lives for her well-being, safety and deliverance), and the images of the violated, suffering Mother-female, become powerful, consolidating and iconic forces for the production of nationalist discourses and acts.

In the period of and surrounding the Revolution, the suffering Mother figure also shades into other variants that incorporate the motifs of ideal womanhood and ideal nationhood so that they become almost synonymous with each other. In the Julis, Sisas, Maria Claras and other images of idealized but afflicted Filipino womanhood, a common denominator exists in the form of the stance of anguished martyrdom, resignation, unhingement or eternal waiting they take—a passivity that feminist scholars have pointed out contrasts sharply with other pictures of female identity retrieved from studies of precolonial women's roles. These latter were carried out with vigor and filled with the self-determining vitality of women actively involved as *babaylanes, catalonans, mambunongs,* storytellers, healers, warriors and epic chanters in the political, economic and spiritual life cycles of their communities.

Under a colonial system which shifts the balance of gender and power relations, the poet-priestess becomes a derivative and debased figure who functions in a symbolic way in areas delegated "safe" for her within the new order: in church, for instance, she no longer presides over spiritual rituals, but dispenses only a decorative role in tasks like the making and laying of altar cloths and the attendance upon priests and laity. And within the circuits of a culture that privileges intellectual and artistic production as primarily male activities and in a corollary move designates the female to the realm of the domestic, the conflation of the images of virgin, madonna, martyr, and suffering mother become most useful for the purposes of promoting an attitude of general submission to the status quo and assuring the continued dominance of social control systems unfavorable to women.

Reading the contemporary Irish poet Eavan Boland, whose meditations on the ways her own struggle to come to terms with Irish history, identity and concepts of nationhood have illuminated what she had considered her heretofore ambivalent and largely undefined feelings about her relationship as a woman, as an Irish woman, and as a poet, to the images of womanhood and Irishness in Irish poetic tradition—I find some important parallels that have to do with the uses of icons or images of the feminine in relation to projects of broad or national representations. An important question is this: how does this impossible feat get achieved by an iconic image like the suffering *Inang Bayan*—"to be at once an archive of defeat, and a diagram of victory"? (Boland)

The association of the national with the feminine does not occur in isolation nor only in the context of Philippine literary history. It occurs not only in the Ireland of which Eavan Boland speaks, but also in the context of other historical and literary traditions the world over. Boland relates in an essay called "Outside History" (which is directly related to the themes developed in a volume of poems bearing the same title) how as a young student at Trinity College, she went to the Isle of Achill off Ireland on an Easter writing retreat or holiday. There, she had the gift of time and leisure, and the use of a friend's cottage. She had also brought with her a pocket edition of "the court poets of the Silver Age" for reading and inspiration. The cottage was unheated and had no plumbing, but every evening an Irish woman from the village below, clad in a rough cardigan and with a tea-towel wrapped around her waist, would carry a bucket of water to her and stop to talk about the people in the community and of the famine ravaging the countryside that season. The woman would tell Boland over and over again how she felt about the tenacity and inner resources of their suffering people. "She kept repeating to me that they were great people, the people in the famine. Great people. I had never heard that before . . . the villages in the famines, she told me, had moved closer to the shore, the better to eat the seaweed."

That encounter was not unduly memorable for Boland, and she did not feel a particular connection with the Achill woman—at least, not immediately. She writes, ". . . when she gestured towards that shore which had stones as outlines and monuments of a desperate people—what was she pointing at? History? A nation? Her memories or mine?" But as the years passed and as Eavan Boland continued to work on her poetry, she found the image of the Achill woman returning to her at the oddest of times. Returning in her imagination to interrogate her younger self, she asks: "Why . . . do you do it? Why do you go back . . . to write in forms explored and sealed by English men hundreds of years ago? You are Irish. You are a woman. Why do you keep these things at the periphery of the poem? Why do you not move them to the center, where they belong?. . . But the woman who looks back at me is uncomprehending. If she answers at all it will be with the rhetoric of a callow apprenticeship; that the poem is pure process, that the technical encounter is the one which guarantees all others . . ."

Because, rereading Irish poets purportedly writing about Irishness, Boland finds that a typical conceit is to evoke nation by means of female folk figures like Dark Rosaleen or Cathleen ni Houlihan; figures made to stand replaceably, one for the other: "The nation as woman; the woman as national muse." The difficulty for her was that now, the more real, flesh-and-blood image of that woman from Achill long ago would rise more vividly in her mind—with her chapped hands, her poverty and her obstinate optimism—more convincing than the romantic, poetic evocations of the emblematic Irish woman-nation.

Like many of our own women of letters who scoured literary history out of a need to see where they could locate themselves within existing poetic traditions, Boland found that even when the majority of early [and mostly male] published writers included women in their texts, they were mostly seen as passive, decorative or symbolic elements, "especially . . . where the woman and the idea of nation were mixed."

Perceptively, Boland is unable to accept these iconic and mythic renditions of female images. Despite their "elevation" to the status of icon, these images are also somehow corruptions because they flatten the image and simplify it by glossing over its original connections to a world of "suffered truth" and reality. The *Inang Bayan* in chains, the Pieta-like figures of suffering women receiving the fallen bodies of dead sons or mates in battle, though they might orginally have arisen from the truth and blood of historical situations, can and have been fashioned into powerful evocatory pictures; but it is also true that without vigilance, they run the risk of collaborating with the very forces that have worked to simplify the position of women in history and in literary tradition.

Their passivity, dependence and suffering can be turned into yet another set of decorative markers that substitute for the sign of femaleness; and when this is conflated with the sign of the nation, how can the project of not only writing my own womanhood in poetry, but also of continuing to write the broader stories of other womanhoods like or unlike mine in their particular, lived historical nuances and specificities—under a compassionate and accommodating tradition of poetic witness—continue fruitfully?

Perhaps these were the same considerations which I instinctively grappled with during those occasions when it seemed I was being made to stand (or speak, as the case may be) as mouthpiece for or representative of some sort, for an idea of womanhood or nationality beyond my own particularized experiences of the same. How does one traverse the treacherous depths between the humanity of individual voicings, and the necessarily simplifying diagrams that are made in the desire for a closer solidarity with others?

The Radical Feminine/The Revolutionary Feminine

To be a woman, and to write; what are the things that inform such a complex project? It is complex enough already that one is what she is—a woman, a Filipino woman, a third world woman, bearing in her life and consciousness the marks not only of her sex and gender but also those of economics and class—and that she is also continually represented in narrative time and space in forms and guises that for a long time she had no way of accessing except through the eyes and words of others. The images we have of ourselves as women existing in real time and history are images that we search for in order to validate and interrogate our individual and collective quests for voice and for identity. But when we turn to history, no less our literary history, it would seem that there has for a long time been a dearth of stories about ourselves, and we hunger for a more complete telling.

My friend Marj Evasco, who is also a poet, feminist scholar and teacher, writes that a survey of Philippine poetry anthologies from 1910 to 1983 shows a very lean harvest of published women's writing over more than seven decades. The 1910 to 1962 *Doveglion Book of Philipine Poetry in English*, edited by Jose Garcia Villa and published by Alberto Florentino, had the "the ratio of three women poets to nineteen male poets." Leonard Casper's 1954 collection *Six Filipino Poets* had only one woman poet out of the six; Emmanuel Torres, *1965-1974 Anthology of Poems* listed five women poets to thirty-three male poets. The Philippine Literary Arts Council published an anthology of nine women poets in 1983.

It is only in recent years that publishing ventures have sought to address this need for a fuller representation of women's voices and narratives in Philippine letters, both here and abroad. Between Ateneo Univeristy Press's decade-apart (1985-1995) publication of two special issues of the journal *Philippine Studies* entitled "New Writing from the Philippines," there has been a more coeval representation of women's writing. Newspaper publisher, editor, poet and fictionist Alfred Yuson has done the same for a special issue of Philippine writing that he edited for the Hawaii-based literary journal *Hawaii* (there is another issue forthcoming late this year). Then there is *Returning a Borrowed Tongue* edited by Nick Carbo (Coffee House Press, 1996); *Brown River White Ocean* editor Luis Francia has also done the same for his anthology, and for a special issue of Philippine poetry he edited for the New York artists and writers magazine *Bomb* (Fall 1993).

In 1992 in the Philippines, Anvil brought out Tina Cuyugan's pathbreaking *Forbidden Fruit: Women Write the Erotic*—the Philippines' first published anthology of women's erotic writing ever. In the same year, Marjorie Evasco and Benilda Santos published their bilingual collection of women's love poetry, *Kung Ibig Mo [If You Desire,* Anvil]. Younger poets like Evasco, Santos, Merlie Alunan Wenceslao, Grace Monte de Ramos, Elizabeth Lolarga, Rowena Tiempo Torrevillas, Merlinda Bobis, Lina Sagaral Reyes, Ruth Elynia Mabanglo and Fatima Lim Wilson published their individual collections.

Then there are the fictions of Lakambini Sitoy, Cristina Pantoja-Hidalgo, Rosario Garcellano, Rosario Cruz Lucero, Joi Barrios, and here in the U.S. Jessica Hagedorn, Ninotchka Rosca, Marianne Villanueva, Cecilia Manguerra Brainard, Michelle Cruz Skinner, and lately, Evelina Galang; and Arlene J. Chai (in Australia). More recently, Edna Manlapaz and Marjorie Evasco published an illuminating volume called *Six Women Poets; Inter-views* in which they conduct conversations shedding intimate light on matters of life, art and craft, with six "matriarchs" in the history of Philippine poetry by women: Angela Manalang Gloria, Trinidad Tarrosa Subido, Edith Tiempo, Virginia Moreno, Tita Lacambra Ayala and Ophelia Dimalanta.

In these collections, these women claim full force the voice which has collectively been silenced for so long, or rendered "safe" and innocuous through social and historical dictates. But though there are gains that we can mark and celebrate today, we also have to remember the women writers in our history who have not had access to the printed word, especially those who have chosen to write vernacular literature. Of our earliest women writers, like Leona Florentino who wrote in the late 1800s in the Ilokos and Magdalena Jalandoni, who in the early 1900s wrote in Hiligaynon, we have only a few surviving fragments of their work. Like women of their time who dared to display and articulate their intellect and wit, they suffered the fate of isolation and social criticism.

And there are also the women in indigenous societies, the women from peasant and working classes, the women from urban poor communities, who also have songs and stories to tell but who traditionally have not had much opportunity to bring their expressions to the attention of a broader audience. It is partly this latter group from which I will be drawing some examples in this paper, to continue the theme of how contemporary women writing poetry in the Philippines today, even when they are not writing directly about the revolution or the revolutionary period or including references to revolutionary female figures, are still by their own praxis continuing and furthering the tradition of bearing across icons of revolutionary Filipina womanhood.

The recuperation of female identity and the revisioning of women's history through writing—which is also the recuperation of identity as female in a very specific kind of cultural matrix (Filipino, third world) are tasks that bristle with risks, especially if the writing openly or unwittingly transgresses existing ethical norms and moral codes of behavior. They also bear witness to and indemnify the idea of how impossible it is to erect clean and entirely separable divisions between "art" and "life." These in themselves radicalize and revolutionize the task of writing women's experiences in poetry.

What is interesting now is that those areas and subjects in writing that were traditionally feminized and given a negative value (i.e. if men wrote about war it was considered important, and if women write about love and relationships or the domestic sphere these were considered trivial concerns), are precisely those areas from which we can speak and write with the most power and force. As Elaine Showalter has noted in a similar vein, in terms of the larger project of synthesizing feminist experience in literature: "One way of writing [our] history . . . would be to situate it in women's time—that is, to emphasize its specificity by narrating its development in terms of internal relationships, continuities, friendships, and institutions."

And so, through our writing and words that spring always from our lives, it is our intensely lived personal circumstances through which we women writers wield the acts of reflection and imagination to produce writing that speaks on several levels—the personal, the communal, the political and the philosophical. The poet Audre Lorde speaks words that apply to the Filipino woman's condition: we, too, must clarify our identity and work for greater empowerment through language, writing and poetry, celebrate our erotic responses to life, cultural experiences, our relationships with our mothers, daughters, sisters and mates, and our need to witness to the daily "small deaths/in the gutter/that are unmaking us all."

Writing our literature is not only a revisioning of our history, but also a strategy for our survival; it becomes, especially in the writing of women's singular and plural identities, a perpetual struggle to rise above everything that is forbidden, bounded, contained, relegated to the realm of the invisible—and as Helene Cixous is keen to perceive, writing is like loving: it is a means, an act for keeping alive, for "leaving no space for death."

ABOUT THE AUTHORS

Valorie Slaughter Bejarano was born in Cebu, Philippines and grew up in the Los Angeles Filipino community. A self-proclaimed "Temple Street Brat," she attended Belmont High School and UCLA. Writing and performing her work for over 15 years, she has been published in *Urthkin, Electrum, Misc. Magazine, Ang Katipunan,* and *Making Waves: An Anthology by and About Asian American Women.* She has written two chapbooks, *Ladies First* and *Before the Sun Comes Up.* Valorie co-wrote and produced two poetry shows: *Voices from the Other Side of the Wall* and *Lovers Make the Worst Ex-husbands.* In November 1989, she was the only Asian woman and Los Angeles poet to perform with the celebrity cast of the Hollywood Women's Political Committee's Pro-Choice rally in Rancho Park as a representative of Asian Pacifics for Choice.

Cecilia Manguerra Brainard is the author and editor of seven books including *When the Rainbow Goddess Wept, Acapulco at Sunset and Other Stories, Philippine Woman in America,* and *Woman With Horns and Other Stories.* She edited *Fiction by Filipinos in America* and

Contemporary Fiction by Filipinos in America and two children's books. In 1998, she received the Outstanding Individual Award from her birth city, Cebu, Philippines. She has also received a California Arts Council Fellowship in Fiction, a Los Angeles Cultural Grant, a Brody Arts Fund Award, and a Special Recognition Award from the Los Angeles City Board of Education for her work dealing with Asian American youths. She has lectured at various institutions including the University of California-Los Angeles, University of Connecticut, California State University-Fullerton, USIS and the University of the Philippines. She teaches creative writing at the Writers' Program at UCLA-Extension.

Susan Evangelista has degrees from Swarthmore College. She first went to the Philippines in 1963 as a member of the Peace Corps. After completing a graduate degree at the University of Wisconsin, she returned to the Philippines with her husband. For the last thirteen years, Susan has been teaching at the Ateneo de Manila University. She has also completed a second graduate degree with a concentration in Asian Studies at the University of the Philippines. Her graduate thesis was on Caros Bulosan. In recent years, she has explored the area of creative writing.

Rosita G. Galang received her Master of Arts in Teaching English as a Second Language from the University of Hawaii and her Ph.D. in Linguistics from the Ateneo de Manila University-Philippine Normal College Consortium. Presently, she is Professor and Chairperson of the Department of International and Multicultural Education at the University of San Francisco. She served as lecturer at the

Summer Institutes for Advanced Research on Asian Americans held at the University of California, Berkeley (1979), Boston University (1980), and the University of Hawaii (1981). Her teaching and research interests include language and culture; language use, acquisition, and teaching; language maintenance and language shift; theoretical and pedagogical aspects of bilingualism and bilingual education; and Filipino American education.

Luisa A. Igloria is a poet, fictionist, and essayist who has previously published five books under the name Maria Luisa A. Cariño: *Cordillera Tales* (New Day, 1990), *Cartography* (Anvil, 1992), *Encanto* (Anvil, 1994), *In the Garden of the Three Islands* (Moyer Bell/Asphodel, 1995), and *Blood Sacrifice* (University of the Philippines Press, 1997). She has been the recipi-ent of numerous grants plus honors including Palanca Awards, 1998 Illinois Arts Council Award, a Fulbright fellowship and National Book Award from the Manila Critics Circle. Luisa's work has appeared in journals like *Poetry, TriQuarterly, Blackwater Review, Hayden's Ferry Review, The Asian Pacific American Journal., Span, Ruptures, Bomb,* and *Black Warrior Review.* She has taught with the University of the Philippines, De La Salle University, and the University of Illinois at Chicago. Originally from Baguio, she is currently with the faculty of the English Department and the Institute for the Study of Minority Issues at Old Dominion University in Norfolk, Virginia.

Paulino Lim, Jr. is Professor of English at California State University, Long Beach. Born in the Philippines, he earned a bachelor's degree in Education and a master's in English at the University of Santo Tomas in Manila, and a doctorate in English at the University of California in Los Angeles. He is the author of a scholarly monograph,

The Style of Lord Byron's Plays; a short fiction anthology, *Passion Summer and Other Stories;* and a quartet of political novels: *Tiger Orchids on Mount Mayon, Sparrows Don't Sing in the Philippines, Requiem for a Rebel Priest,* and *Ka Gaby, Nom de Guerre.*

Edmundo F. Litton, originally from Manila, is an Assistant Professor in the School of Education at Loyola Marymount University, Los Angeles. Prior to his faculty appointment he served as Director of Asian and Pacific Students Services at LMU. He completed a Master of Arts in Teaching degree at Georgetown University. He also holds a MA in Educational Technology and a Doctorate in

Education from the University of San Francisco. Prior to emigrating to the United States, he was a high school teacher in the Philippines with the La Salle Brothers. In the United States, he has worked with the Filipino community as an elementary school teacher and a teacher educator. His research interests include issues relating to cultural diversity, Catholic education, teacher preparation, educational technology and educational issues in the Filipino community.

Herminia Meñez was born in Kalibo, Aklan. She received her undergraduate and graduate degrees in English literature from St. Scholastica's College in Manila and from the Dominican College of San Rafael, California. Her Doctorate of Philosophy degree in Folklore and Folklife is from the

University of Pennsylvania. She taught folklore and ethnic studies for nearly twenty years at California State University, Sonoma and retired as Professor of American Multicultural Studies in 1989. Early retirement has allowed her to do what she enjoys most: spending time with her husband, Stanley Coben, Professor of United States history at UCLA, working out on the UCLA track or walking along Ocean Boulevard in Santa Monica discussing their research and writing. Her most recent book is *Explorations in Philippine Folklore* (Ateneo de Manila University Press, 1996).

Susan N. Montepio has a B.A. in English and an M.A. in Anthropology from the University of the Philippines. She has a Certificate in the Teaching of English as a Second Language and an M.A. in Folklore and Mythology from the University of California Los Angeles (UCLA). Her paper is based on her dissertation research which focused on the creative activities of Filipino American senior citizens in Norwalk, California.

Elizabeth Pastores-Palffy is Professor and Faculty Advisor at The Union Institute College of Undergraduate Studies, Los Angeles, California. She has a Doctor of Philosophy degree in History from the University of California, Los Angeles. She has taught courses in History in the Philippines and in the United States. She has also presented papers at numerous conferences.

E. San Juan, Jr. is Professor and Chair of the Department of Comparative American Cultures, Washington State University. After receiving his Ph. D. in English and Comparative Literature from Harvard University, he taught at the University of California,

University of Connecticut, Brooklyn College, University of the Philippines, and elsewhere. His recent books are *Beyond Postcolonial Theory* and *From Exile to Diaspora: Versions of the Filipino Experience in the U.S.A.* He was recently awarded a Centennial Award for achievement in literature by the Cultural Center of the Philippines.

Felice Prudente Sta. Maria is an awarded writer and an advocate of cultural environment development for values education. She is president of Atocha Alternatives, vice-chair of Metropolitan Museum of Manila, commissioner (to retool historic sites) of Philippine Centennial Commission, and vice-chair for the Human and Social Sciences Committee of UNESCO National Commission of the Philippines. She received the rank of Chevalier in the Grand Ordre des Artes et Letres from the Republic of France in 1990.

Nadine Sarreal studied applied mathematics at the University of the Philippines. Secretly, through her childhood and early adulthood, she wrote notebooks of poetry and stories. Nadine is married and has two children. She decided, five years ago, to come out of the closet (or out from under the bedsheets where she had been writing with the aid of a flashlight) and be a writer in public. She studied creative writing under the Vermont College MFA program. She has had two books of poetry published and several stories included in Filipino-American literary anthologies. At this time, Nadine is working on a collection of short stories and trying really hard to write a novel.

Santiago Sia is Professor of Philosophy at Loyola Marymount University, Los Angeles. He was also the Director of Asian and Pacific Studies (1990-1996) at LMU. He has taught in universities and colleges in the Philippines, Ireland, England and Belgium and other countries and is the recipient of a number of awards and fellowships from various academic institutions. He has published several scholarly books and articles as well as a novel, *The Fountain Arethuse* (Lewes, UK: The Book Guild, 1997). He is presently writing another novel set mainly in the Philippines and Ireland.

John L. Silva is the son of Ilonggo and Ilocano parents. He migrated to the United States in 1971. A vocal critic of the Marcos dictatorship, Silva was included in the infamous "black list" of eighty US-based Filipinos, preventing Silva from returning to the Philippines at the time. While in exile, Silva opposed the Marcos regime's human rights violations and wrote many articles denouncing Marcos and his policies. Silva earned his MA in Philippine-American History at Goddard Cambridge. He has worked as the executive director of GCHP, a San Francisco-based organization that managed education and health care programs among Asian and Pacific Islanders infected with HIV. Silva has done advocacy work for increased AIDS funding. He was also former associate publisher and advertising director of US-based *Filipinas Magazine*. In 1996, Silva returned to the Philippines to manage the Geronimo Berenguer de los Reyes Foundation Museum.

Ruel S. de Vera was born in 1973 in Quezon City and graduated from the Ateneo de Manila University with a degree in Communications as a scholar of the *Philippine Daily Inquirer*. He is a staffwriter for the *Sunday Inquirer Magazine*. He teaches journalism at the Ateneo's Department of Communications. He has three books from Anvil Publishing, *The Most Careful of Stars: Poems, The Spirit Quest Chronicles Book 1* and *Book 2*. He has won awards for his writing and was nominated for the national book award. He edits for the literary journal *Pen & Ink*. He has written for *Metro Magazine* and *Asiaweek*. He attended the 1997 Yale-China American Studies Summer Institute for Asian Scholars at Yale University.

Damon Lawrence Woods grew up in Baguio City, the son of missionary parents. He received a Ph.D. in Southeast Asian History from the University of California, Los Angeles. He has taught at UCLA and is currently a visiting lecturer at the University of California, Irvine, where he teaches different aspects of Southeast Asian history, including a course on the Philippine Radical Tradition. His dissertation examined Tomas Pinpin's *Librong pagaaralan nang manga Tagalog nang Uicang Castila.* His research continues to focus on indigenous language sources.